Irish

IN WISCONSIN

David G. Holmes

THE WISCONSIN HISTORICAL SOCIETY PRESS

Madison

Published by the
Wisconsin Historical Society Press
© 2004 by The State Historical Society of Wisconsin

Photographs identified with PH, WHi, or WHS are from the Society's collections; address inquiries about such photos to the Visual Materials Archivist at the above address.

Publications of the Wisconsin Historical Society Press are available at quantity discounts for promotions, fund raising, and educational use. Write to the above address for more information.

Printed in the United States of America
Designed by Jane Tenenbaum
Photo research by John Nondorf
The following excerpt has been reprinted with permission: *"The Body of an American"* by Shane McGowan.

Publication of this book was made possible in part by a gift from the Milwaukee Irish Fest Foundation, Inc. Additional funding was provided by a grant from the Alice E. Smith Fellowship fund.

07 06 05 04 03   5 4 3 2 1

Library of Congress Cataloging-in-Publication Data
Holmes, David G.
  Irish in Wisconsin / David G. Holmes.
    p. cm.
  Includes bibliographical references and index.
  ISBN 0-87020-346-0 (pbk. : alk. paper)
  1. Irish Americans—Wisconsin—History. 2. Immigrants—Wisconsin—History.
  3. Wisconsin—Ethnic relations. 4. Wisconsin—Emigration and immigration—History.
  5. Ireland—Emigration and immigration—History. I. Title.
F590.I6H65 2004
977.5'0049162073—dc22   2004007146

♾ The paper used in this publication meets the minimum requirements of the American National Standard for Information Sciences{m}Permanence of Paper for Printed Library Materials, ANSI Z39.48-1992.

'Ah, Rosaleen, ye're sad again Like ould Erin you're sad when you're cheerful, and you smile wid the tears in your eyes.'

ACKNOWLEDGMENTS

I would like to recognize the editorial staff of the Wisconsin Historical Society who certainly improved this book with their suggestions and advice, specifically Margaret Dwyer. However, I am solely responsible for any errors of omission or commission that remain. I also want to thank my family and friends, who have provided not only support but intellectual insight as well.

I wish to dedicate this book to my wife Laura and my daughter Elizabeth.

David G. Holmes
April 2004

The Irish in Wisconsin, 1870

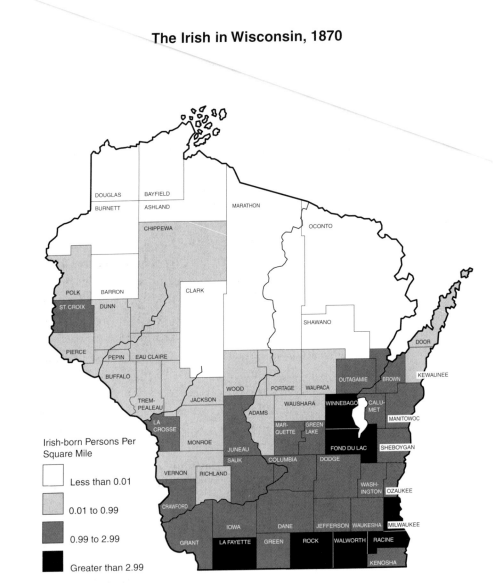

Irish-born Persons Per
Square Mile

Less than 0.01

0.01 to 0.99

0.99 to 2.99

Greater than 2.99

Map by Joel Heiman

FOREWORD
by Tommy Makem

Readers may find it surprising to see my name on the foreword of a book about Wisconsin history. I was surprised myself at the request from the Wisconsin Historical Society. Although I have been to Milwaukee and other cities in Wisconsin many times over the years, it does seem odd to ask me, a native of Armagh, and long-time resident of Dover, New Hampshire, to share my thoughts about the history of Irish people in the Badger State.

When I learned, however, that this book was going to introduce each of its topical sections with lyrics from different traditional and contemporary Irish songs, I began to understand how this story, although it happens a long way from the places I know so well personally, is a universal one. I did know from the many different ethnic festivals that occur every summer on Milwaukee's lakefront that Wisconsin's residents hold dear a strong immigrant background. I go every August to celebrate with the Irish-American community, but I am also aware that people of German, Italian, Polish, and many other backgrounds spend a few days every summer celebrating their ethnic traditions. Other than that, I didn't know too much about the Irish in Wisconsin until I read a draft of the manuscript.

The book begins on familiar turf, describing the history of Ireland, and explaining why so many needed to leave home. All immigrant stories start there, with a reason to leave. Various reasons to leave Ireland have existed throughout history, but the famine, the great hunger, *An Gorta Mór*, is the one that brought so many to Wisconsin in the mid-nineteenth century. You may know in my song, "Four Green Fields" the lines, ". . . 'my children starved by mountain, valley, and sea, and their wailing cries, they shook the very heavens, my four green fields ran red with their blood,' said she. . . ."

The Irish who came to Wisconsin in the highest number came in the years during and immediately after the famine, and the fertile fields and the primeval forests must have seemed a salvation.

They had to make the journey first, of course. Certainly the number of songs about leaving Ireland, about saying goodbye and making the journey, could fill hours, even days of listening time. The journey is the second part of every immigration story, and in the nineteenth century there was only one way to go, by water. Water, for an island country like Ireland, has always had special meaning, but in the nineteenth century a trip across the Atlantic would likely be one-way. For a people that often did not stir outside of their home county, America could have been the moon. "Danny Boy" might have evolved into a cliché over time, but beneath the sentiment is a father acknowledging that if his beloved son should ever return, it's more likely that he himself will be "in the meadow" rather than alive to greet him.

It is the third part of the story, the arriving and the settling, that becomes less universal, and more sculpted by the destination itself. It is in this book that readers will learn how the Irish in the 1840s through the 1860s were often more populous in the census rolls than the Germans. Like the Germans, the newly arrived Irish immigrants formed their own regiment during the Civil War, the Wisconsin Seventeenth, although some ugly scenes related to the draft did occur. And it was politics in the Civil War era that led to the *Lady Elgin* disaster, when so many of Milwaukee's political leaders, at that time heavily Irish, were lost in Lake Michigan when the *Lady Elgin* was struck and sank near Winnetka, Illinois. If the *Lady Elgin* tale sounds familiar, it may be because there is a song about it. In the pages that follow, readers can ponder how different the history of the Irish in Wisconsin might have been if those leaders had not been lost, and if the city of Milwaukee, which came to be known as the "German Athens" for its large number of German residents and leaders, might have had a more distinctive Celtic profile.

For the history of the Irish in Wisconsin did change as the nineteenth century progressed. The number of Irish-born immigrants who lived in Wisconsin dropped with each decade's census as waves of groups from northern and central European countries flooded the state. Agrarian communities that dotted Wisconsin with names like Erin Prairie soon gave way to new names and new identities. It would be easy to theorize that the story ends in the late nineteenth century. But the Irish, although they grew less visible, continued to make history in Wisconsin.

In 1874, Edward G. Ryan was made State Supreme Court Justice, and this native of Ireland was the leading voice of justice in the state until his death. The Cudahy family embraced a distinctive Wisconsin trade and entered into the meat packing business. Although few songs in my repertoire comment on either the courtroom or the cattle pen, I do sing a number of songs about everyday life and small but important moments. That perhaps is the best description of the ongoing history of the Irish in Wisconsin. The community here has not chosen to converge publicly in ways like the Irish-Americans in New England or New York. But those who remained and put down roots did not give up their traditional expressions of faith, or family structures, or ways of celebrating and remembering.

In the 1990 federal census, the government began asking for respondents to identify their ethnic backgrounds. It came as a shock to many who had studied the ethnic trends of Wisconsin that the Irish were the second largest group among those who provided the information. The census returns coincide with a strong wave of Celtic and Irish pride, and perhaps identifying oneself as Irish is almost a fad. But readers of this book will find that the Irish in Wisconsin experienced a vibrant history, and its quieter, less visible nature than that of communities in the northeastern United States, give the state of Wisconsin another unique story to tell.

In the pages ahead, David Holmes offers readers a great deal of historical information, but I will leave you with a more poetic thought about leaving home and finding it again.

Life Waters

The Celtic gods of sun and water set a river flowing
Of music and of poetry and wisdom past all knowing.
The bards and druids drank their fill, the brehon's sons and daughters,
The fili, too, refreshed their souls with these sweet mystic waters.

And time grew old, and times grew dark, the river seemed forsaken,
A chosen few would now partake, where many had partaken.
And other races found our forebears' wisdom well worth learning,
Their ancient songs and poetry touched hearts for ever yearning.

Now, aeons passed, on distant shores, far from the holy mountain,
The sons of sons re-found the source and built a flowing fountain
Of music and of poetry and wisdom from those waters
To soothe the parched and weary souls of all our sons and daughters.

INTRODUCTION

When the federal government released the results of the census for the year 2000, the percentage of people in Wisconsin who claimed Irish ancestry was approximately 11 percent. This seemingly low statistic caused quite a stir. Although census reports are always important with their potential for redistricting and reapportioning, the state's news agencies covered the statistics on ethnicity extensively. Of the many European nationalities to settle in Wisconsin, the Germans, Scandinavians, and Slavs have put a face on Wisconsin's popular culture and history. Images of German bratwurst and beer are found in city bars and village taverns, the ubiquitous Swiss cheese head appears everywhere the Packers play, and traditional polka dancers sport colorful Polish costumes. Although the Irish have been present in Wisconsin since European settlement began in the early nineteenth century, in contrast to their impact on the culture of cities on the East Coast, their influence here appears to be of minor importance when compared to that of other ethnic groups.

That is, until 11 percent of Wisconsin citizens identified themselves as Irish in the 2000 census, making Irish ancestry second only to German, and edging out the Norwegians and Poles (both at 9 percent), as well as the English, French, Italian, Dutch, Czech, and Swedish, all of whom reported at 7 percent or less. These statistical results do not change either popular impressions or historic evidence, of course, especially since the option of identifying one's racial and ethnic background has only existed since the 1980 census. What made the statistics newsworthy was the challenge to the state's sense of ethnic identity, the suggestion that another story needed to be added to those that have been prevalent for so long. The Irish contribution to the state's history and culture reveals itself to be more important than earlier impressions indicate. Even if the story of the Irish in Wisconsin proves to be a comparatively minor one, it is a story worth telling, because within the larger history of Irish immigration into the United States, the Wisconsin chapter is a multifaceted and intriguing chronicle that adds much to the Irish experience in America.

The last time the Irish placed second in the Wisconsin census was in

1860. However, as the nineteenth century moved into the twentieth, the Irish flavor in Wisconsin began to fade for various reasons. Fewer new immigrants from Ireland came to live in the state. Also, many sons and daughters of Irish immigrants moved out of the state for economic or family reasons. Finally, many descendants of the Irish in Wisconsin began identifying themselves primarily with the United States or Wisconsin, leaving behind, as other second- and third-generation immigrants did, the traditions of their ancestors. Today, however, there is a resurgence of interest in Irish music, dancing, athletics, history, literature, language, and genealogy throughout the state, throughout the year, culminating in one giant party every August on Milwaukee's lakefront.

The Smithsonian Institution's National Folk Life program has deemed Milwaukee's Irish Fest the "largest and best Irish cultural event in North America." At Irish Fest there is good food, music, conversation, and a general celebratory atmosphere. Each Irish Fest has a theme, such as famine or exile, and these themes lend the festival a deeper level of exploration of Irish culture than would be found in a typical ethnic carnival. Educational booths are set up to inform people about Irish history and literature, and to provide lessons in the Irish language. A genealogical display offers computerized help to people who want to find out more about their Irish ancestors. The music on stage offers both traditional and contemporary Irish music and is accompanied by traditional Irish dancing. The Trinity Irish Dance Company, which often performs at the Fest, has won international awards for the interpretive skills of their dancers and choreographers. In short, this festival offers more than food and dance. The annual celebration attracts approximately one hundred thousand visitors, and although many come from outside the state, at its core it is truly a Wisconsin experience.

The pride of heritage that contributes to the success of Irish Fest and all of the celebrations of Irish traditions has its roots in the history of Irish settlement in Wisconsin. In order to fully understand this history, it is first necessary to place that history within a larger context. Why did the Irish emigrate from their native land and why did they come to Wisconsin? Once we explore the answers to these questions we will have a better understanding of the immigrants' beliefs, prejudices, expectations, and motivations.

EXILES OF ERIN

I'm bidding you a long farewell My Mary,
*   kind and true*
But I'll not forget you, darling
In the land I'm going to
They say there's bread and work for all
And the sun shines always there
But I'll not forget old Ireland
Were it fifty times as fair

"Lament of the Irish Immigrant," Traditional

Irish immigration to the United States began before there was a United States. Not long after the English colonies were established, people from Ireland began to arrive on these shores. These seventeenth-century Irish immigrants, many of whom came to be known as the Scots-Irish, were quite different from those who arrived later, during the famine years. The factors that caused these early immigrants to move were unlike the factors influencing later groups, and they came from different socioeconomic and religious backgrounds, as well. These fundamental differences between pre-1845 immigrants and those that arrived afterward reflected divisions within Ireland itself. These divisions were the result of English rule and its impact upon the emigrants' homeland.

The relationship between the islands of Great Britain and Ireland is a complex one, but a basic understanding of that relationship allows greater understanding of the immigrant story. Great Britain ruled all of Ireland for most of the seventeenth century through the beginning of the twentieth century. Prior to 1800, Ireland did have its own parliament, subordinate to the monarch and parliament in England, a situation that caused Irish partisans to make various attempts to break free of British control. After an unsuccessful rebellion in 1798, the British Crown instituted the union of Great Britain and Ireland in 1800 to ensure against similar political agitation in the future. Ireland still elected members to parliament, but those members sat in the British Parliament because Britain had abolished the Irish parliament. The British attempt to quash rebellion through more hands-on control of the country did not work. Irish patriots continued to attempt to liberate Ireland from its more powerful neighbor's control, and they eventually succeeded in 1921. With the leadership of men like Eamonn De Valera and Michael Collins and through the use of guerilla tactics, the Irish were finally able to force Britain's hand on independence. Parliament had considered Home Rule for Ireland (a form of political independence) in the decades prior to this Irish War of Independence, but it became clear that the Northern part of Ireland, Ulster, would be a sticking point. After 1921, Northern Ireland remained under British rule and does to this day. The reason for the North's special treatment revolves around the religion and politics of earlier centuries.

Irish nationalism was defined as a movement to win self-governance for Ireland, and religion was a main factor in why Irish nationalists wanted to sever ties with Great Britain. The population of England, Scotland, and Wales was overwhelmingly Protestant, whereas the Irish population was overwhelmingly Catholic. Rebellions in the seventeenth century convinced the British government to place various restrictions on the Catholic population in Ireland and to take a more hands-on approach to governance there. Catholics were pushed off their land to make room for a mass influx of Protestant settlers. The province of Ulster, in the North of Ireland, which once belonged to the strongest and most rebellious Irish leaders, became home to most of these Protestant settlers. Further hardships for Catholics came as a result of the Penal Laws, which were passed in phases, first in 1695, then in 1704. These laws restricted Catholics' rights to education and to bear arms, and individuals had to essentially renounce their religion in order to hold public office. Laws pertaining to land inheritance meant that Catholics gradually lost ownership of their land, and the result was that Protestant landlords ended up owning the vast majority of Ireland. Further legislation in 1728 removed voting rights for Catholics. Because Protestants in Ireland owed their land and power to the efforts of the British Crown, they generally remained loyal to the union of Great Britain and Ireland. Catholics, on the other hand, yearned to be free of British rule.

Yet, not all Protestants were enamored of British rule. The same colonial restrictions that led the American colonies to rebel also rankled Irish political thinkers. The United Irishmen rebellion of 1798 involved both Catholics and Protestants and its most vocal leaders were actually Protestant. In the seventeenth and eighteenth centuries, the majority of people coming to the American colonies and the United States from Ireland were Protestant. They left for political and economic reasons. Irish Presbyterians left because they did not like paying taxes to support the established Anglican Church. Some fled what they considered a repressive regime to come to a place with a more democratic form of government. Many entrepreneurial types left because they saw more opportunities across the Atlantic. Whatever their reasons, Irish Protestants at that time emigrated from Ireland at a higher rate than their Catholic counterparts. In North America, Protestants from Ireland identified themselves as Irish during the colonial era, then later as Scots-Irish (reflecting the fact that many of the settlers of Ulster came from Scotland). This identification allowed them to differentiate themselves from the massive influx of Irish Catholics that arrived later.

There were a few major factors leading to a lower percentage of Catholics leaving Ireland prior to the nineteenth century. Primarily the typical Catholic was too destitute to consider emigrating. Emigration was costly and Catholics, often landless and growing more indebted to the landlord with every generation, did not have the funds to pay for passage to America. Many did enter into indentured servitude, though, and ultimately a significant number of Catholics, though not as many as the total number of Protestants, arrived on the North American continent in the seventeenth and eighteenth centuries. Yet, the American colonies, like Great Britain, were not receptive to adherents of the Roman Catholic religion. Once here, another problem they faced was the language barrier. At this time the Irish language—often called Gaelic but also referred to as Irish—was the native language of a large percentage of the population. These native Irish speakers often did not speak English. Perhaps most important, Irish Catholics in general were traditional in their outlook. They made their living off the land and the importance of family and homeland was paramount. To leave the place of one's birth and one's family to live in a far-off land would not have been a consideration for most Irish Catholics. For these people, change was something to be feared, until it became unavoidable.

This change began to occur in the late eighteenth and early nineteenth centuries. Anglo-Irish landlords brought modern agricultural techniques into Ireland, and these more efficient methods often meant less land for Irish farmers and less work for Irish agricultural workers. At the same time Ireland was experiencing a population boom that was very rapid even by contemporary European standards. Population doubled in the eighteenth century to approximately five million people, and although the growth rate slowed after 1820, the population of Ireland stood at approximately eight million on the eve of the famine. The fastest growing regions of Ireland were the south and west, which also were the poorest. This demographic development strained resources as more people had to rely on smaller and smaller plots of land. Beginning around 1820, Catholics started to immigrate to North America in larger numbers.

THE GREAT HUNGER

Oh father dear, I oft-times hear you speak of Erin's isle
Her lofty hills, her valleys green, her mountains rude and wild
They say she is a lovely land wherein a saint might dwell
So why did you abandon her, the reason to me tell.
Oh son, I loved my native land with energy and pride
Till a blight came o'er the praties; my sheep, my cattle died
My rent and taxes went unpaid, I could not them redeem
And that's the cruel reason why I left Skibberreen.

"Skibberreen," Traditional

The great famine changed everything in Ireland. Historians talk of pre-famine and post-famine Ireland because the country was so transformed by the event that speaking of Ireland in the nineteenth century is like describing two different countries. In 1845 blight hit the potato crop of Ireland. Three million of Ireland's poorest people were entirely dependent on the potato as their main source of nutrition and another one million were heavily dependent on it as a staple ingredient in cooking. The potato, an excellent source of nutrition, met 60 percent of the food needs of the Irish population on the eve of the famine. Average consumption for these people was on the order of 10–14 lbs of potatoes a day for a man and 8–10 lbs a day for a woman. When this crop failed it brought devastation in its wake. Between 1846 and 1851, approximately one million people died of starvation and disease. Those that died tended to be the poorest people and they lived in the Gaelic-speaking districts of the South and West. Those who were a step up on the socioeconomic ladder were able to emigrate.

Approximately 1.5 million people left Ireland in the decade between 1845–1854, and most of these people came to the United States. The bulk of the Irish population in Wisconsin came from this group of immigrants and those who left the country in the decades before the famine. One of these Irish immigrants was John Lawless. In 1846, his brother Thomas in Termonfeckin, Co. Drogheda, wrote to him in Patch Grove, Grant County of the Wisconsin Territory:

> I really cannot say how we will live in this country. The potato crop has failed in this country this year as it did in 1845, with this difference that the distemper or infection, set in this year about the end of June before the late crop planted in May had time to form; the early ones are very much infected in places and in other parts not so much but the disease is progressing and we all consider that there will not be a potato to put in at November. We have also had great rains and severe gales of wind, which it is feared has injured the corn crops; so that you see there is a poor look out for the ensuing Spring and Summer; should the potato crop fail, as is anticipated, my business falls to the ground.
>
> I have often been inclined especially since Father's death, to go to America but should I make the least move in that way, Jenny would be after me, she would not stay behind, she would leave children and all and follow me, so that you see I am poorly circumstanced. . . .
>
> I may perhaps make up my mind to go to America wither this winter coming on, or in Spring. I cannot yet speak positively on Jenny's account; I might however surprise you by calling to see you before you might be aware of it.

It is not known whether Thomas Lawless emigrated to join his brother. He was writing one year before the worst year of the famine, called Black '47; his prediction of another potato crop failure unfortunately held true.

An event on the magnitude of the Irish famine necessarily changes a society. Consider the fact that in 1846 the population of Ireland was estimated at 8.2 million, while in 2001 the estimated combined population of the Republic of Ireland and Northern Ireland was 5.5 million. Ireland's population growth after the famine stagnated. Learning the economic lessons of the famine and its devastating effects on small landholders and landless laborers, farmers consolidated land and passed on their farms to only one son, often the eldest. Before the famine, land had often been divided among all the sons, leading to small plots that produced little income and little food.

The famine was also a cultural watershed. Before the famine, most Irish were nominally Catholic, but many of the poorest people practiced a type of folk religion that differed from Catholicism. Many Irish held tradition-based beliefs in fairies and banshees and attributed magical properties to certain areas, mountains, wells, and other features of their local landscape. The population boom prior to the eighteenth century along with the Penal Laws and a lack of qualified priests meant that many people in remote areas had no access to formal religion. After the famine, Ireland underwent what historian Emmet Larkin has called a Devotional Revolution. Stronger ties to Rome were developed and a concerted effort to bring official religion to the people was begun. The result was that Ireland's population was more committed to Catholicism and its tenets after the famine. Finally, the famine devastated the Gaeltacht, that area of Ireland where Irish was still the everyday language. The Gaelic language went into a serious decline as a result. Among the losses of the famine were many of the cultural traditions and restrictions that had previously made the Irish Catholic so resistant to emigration.

All these developments led to a society that was deeply conservative. Late marriages and strict sanctions against pre-marital sex complemented Catholic mores but they also helped reign in impulses that could destroy arranged marriages and indirectly lead to familial poverty. Ireland was a country that provided little opportunity to most of its men and women. The large landowners were still overwhelmingly Protestant as were members of the professions. If one was not an eldest son, career choices were limited. A thriving business community did not exist outside of the anomalous North, where religious bigotry meant that most of the good jobs still went to Protestants, and there was no open land on which to set up one's own farm. Many Irish people believed that their only opportunity for a better life lay overseas. William Shea, who left the Dingle Peninsula in Co. Kerry, in 1884 and settled in Osceola in Fond du Lac County, was just such a man. He was not the eldest son and had few prospects for making a decent living. He earned the $70 for passage to America and left. "About all I brought with me was the clothes I was wearing, some stockings and underwear, a knife, fork, tin cup and plate," he wrote. "As we heard the horn of the mailman and stagecoach coming in the distance, Father came and shook hands with me and said, 'Good-bye' and disappeared in the crowd. That was the last I saw of him until I went back to Ireland 25 year later."

It is not an exaggeration to say that, from the famine to the present, Ireland's greatest export has been its people. With a few exceptional periods, Ireland has contributed a steady stream of immigrants for other nations. In the nineteenth century alone, over five million people left Ireland to come to the United States. By 1850, Wisconsin had approximately twenty-one thousand residents who were born in Ireland (6.9 percent of Wisconsin's total population) and in 1860, on the eve of the Civil War, that number had risen to fifty thousand (6.4 percent of the total population—but by then their percentage of total population was declining because of the influx of other ethnic groups, particularly Germans).

❂

JOURNEY

The seas roared in anger, making desperate our plight
And a fever came o'er me that worsened next night
Then delirium possessed me and clouded my mind
And I for a moment saw that land left behind.
I could hear in the distance my dear mother's wailing
And the prayers of three brothers that I'd never see no more
And I felt father's tears as he begged for forgiveness
For seeking a new life on the still distant shore.

"An Emigrant's Daughter," Traditional

During the famine, Irish people journeyed to the United States on "coffin ships," so termed because of their dire reputation. Many of these ships stopped in Canada because inspections of the boats were more lax there than in the United States. Rations were few and unhealthy, ventilation was designed for cargo not human passengers, and the safety of the vessels themselves was highly questionable.

Surviving this treacherous, six- to eight-week journey was difficult enough but fresh hardships greeted the immigrant once he or she touched land. John Solon, who settled in Shields in Dodge County, left

Co. Mayo with his father, mother, and two brothers. His baby brother died after hitting his head while disembarking from the ship. His mother died en route from Albany to Buffalo of a "raging fever" most likely caught onboard the ship, and his older brother died of fever shortly after they settled in Wisconsin. The Solons and many like them risked the dangerous journey because they realized that the United States was their best hope to start a new and more prosperous life.

Most Irish immigrants of the nineteenth century spent some time in the Northeastern and Mid-Atlantic states before moving on to Wisconsin. Their journeys to Wisconsin varied according to the period of their trek. Access to the state was made easier with the coming of the railroad after mid-century, and immigrants like William Shea, who came over in 1884, took advantage of its speed and convenience. Before the expansion of the railroads, the Great Lakes and canals provided access to the Northeastern States, and the Mississippi River in the West connected Wisconsin to the Ohio Valley, the East, St. Louis, and the South. The Solons took the former route. The McGowan family used a combination of rail and waterways to arrive in Milwaukee before taking a wagon over rough roads to journey north to the Township of Warren in Waushara County. The McGowan's were originally going to stay in Ohio, but, "Ohio not proving satisfactory," they pushed on to Wisconsin. Many of these immigrants lived elsewhere for months or years before moving to Wisconsin; the average length of time spent in other states was seven years. At times the destination of the settlers seemed more a matter of chance than choice. Blanche Childs Reardon writes of her ancestors, "A family tradition suggests that they had originally planned to go to Minnesota (after living in Ohio and Illinois). Most likely, it would have been to join the Connollys. However, by the early 1860s the Connollys had moved to Polk County, Wisconsin, and that became the Reardons' and Stapletons' destination." Many of the Irish immigrants who settled in Wisconsin in the 1850s and 1860s, in keeping with this transitory trend, later moved on to other states such as the Dakotas and Minnesota. The Reardon and Stapleton families produced settlers to both those areas after making a home in the St. Croix Valley.

❈

IN AMERICA

I'm bidding farewell to the land of my youth
and the home I love so well.
And the mountains so grand round my own native land,
I'm bidding them all farewell.
With an aching heart I'll bid them adieu
for tomorrow I'll sail far away,
O'er the raging foam for to seek a home
on the shores of Amerikay.
"The Shores of Amerikay," Traditional

Every immigrant group in the United States has its own unique experience and culture. It is important to briefly explain some of the traits characteristic to the Irish experience, because this will illuminate the contribution the Irish made to Wisconsin's development.

A newly arrived Irish immigrant, particularly a Catholic who emigrated before or during the famine, would more than likely identify himself or herself by the locality they came from in Ireland. Familial history was very important to the Irish, and each family had deep roots in their community—roots that local historians often meticulously tracked. The attraction to place meant that great attention was paid to the details of the landscape around one's home. For example, hills, valleys, trees, etc., would be named individually. The provincial outlook of most of these immigrants meant that they had little experience interacting with people outside of their local community. The journey over to the United States or Canada was probably the first time many Irish came into contact with anyone outside their own region. When people from Derry told their experiences to people from Dublin and Waterford and in turn heard of similar joys and tribulations, they realized that these people were truly their compatriots. There is a good chance that a male immigrant arriving in New York would see himself as a Corkman or Kerryman as opposed to an Irishman. However, native-born Americans had little time for such hairsplitting—an Irish person was an Irish person. Discrimination from native-born Americans tended to drive the Irish population closer together, particularly in the large cities of the East Coast. The distinctions between Irish people from different areas began to dissolve under these new circumstances, and it is fair to say that Irish nationalism in Ireland received a boost from this sense of camaraderie fostered in the United States.

Religion was one of the reasons that many native-born Americans did not embrace Irish immigrants. In the early nineteenth century, Catholics outnumbered Protestants as immigrants from Ireland. After the famine that situation was cemented, and when discussion arises about Irish immigration, the discussion centers on Irish Catholics. The ethnic heritage of the white population in the United States in the early to mid-nineteenth century was overwhelmingly Anglo-Saxon. Their religious background and cultural assumptions were similar to the population of Great Britain, the rulers of Ireland. They tended to view Catholicism as a dangerous, anti-democratic religion that promoted ignorance, superstition, and blind obedience. For the Irish, Catholicism increasingly became a badge of national identity. Religion is the reason they were kicked off their land in Ireland and why they had little political power there. Because of the gradual loss of their native language and adoption of the English language, religion became a crucial distinction between an English and an Irish person and Catholicism soon became the main component of Irish identity in this country. The more they were hated and discriminated against because of their religion, the more they clung to it. For Irish immigrants, the Catholic Church was a beacon in a harsh, strange world. Within a short period of their arrival in the United States, they took control of the Catholic Church in this country.

The verses of the Irish folk songs that introduce the chapters of this book share a common theme—exile. Some of the first Irish emigrants were rebel leaders like Hugh O'Neill and Rory O'Donnell, Irish nobility exiled to the European continent by the British in the early seventeenth century. Later, other Irish nationalist leaders like Thomas Francis Meagher and John Mitchell were forced to leave their country because of their opposition to British rule. The average Irish emigrant also viewed himself or herself as an exile. They, like the Irish heroes of song and story, were forced to leave by the cruelty of British rule.

This was the image they presented in song and story, but the reality was different. The Irish emigrant left of his or her own accord. They left to escape a land that offered them little to no opportunity and came to the United States because they believed this country would provide them a better life. However, in recalling the reasons for emigrating, they tended to exaggerate a type of forced exile due to British oppression. Historian Kerby Miller has noted, "[T]here seems no reason inherent in either the actual circumstances of most emigrant's departures or the material condition of Irish-American life which automatically translated a homesickness perhaps common to all emigrants into a morbid perception of themselves as involuntary exiles, passive victims of British oppression." He believes that a "distinctive Irish Catholic worldview rooted deeply in Irish history and culture" was responsible for this exile theme. It could be a debilitating outlook because it took control out of the hands of the immigrant; the immigrant became a passive victim instead of an active participant in his or her own destiny, but it could also turn outward into a strong desire to identify with and aid the land they felt exiled from. It thus meant that hatred for British rule survived among the Irish in America. This worldview is one of the distinguishing characteristics of the Irish immigrant. It is reflected in their strong attachment to the Church, because it was the Church that connected them to their home and the reasons why they left. It was a force behind their involvement in nationalist politics, which focused on Irish independence from British rule. In general, it infused the culture of Irish America.

This culture of exile did not lead the Irish to return to their home country despite overwhelming homesickness. The Irish, more than most any other ethnic group, stayed in the United States rather than returning to their home. Other immigrants from Europe often left their wives and families in their home country while they earned money to help bring them to America. The Irish immigrant experience was also a bit different because of the large number of females that came to America. The number of women and men leaving Ireland after the famine was roughly equal. The high percentage of females is distinctive within European ethnic groups. Many of these women were single, another aspect unique to Irish immigrants, and they left for the same reasons as their male counterparts. This often meant that single Irish men could start families in America with people from their own culture, with whom they felt comfortable.

Because of the strict morality of the Catholic Church and the economic restraints involved in trying to set up successful "matches" for young men and women, many females in Ireland faced a clear lack of choice when it came to their future companionship. Many were destined to remain single their entire lives whether they wanted to or not, and even if they did marry, the groom was often chosen for them. If a woman picked her own mate, it was a decision born of panic. In the United States, Irish women found jobs and often blossomed in the more open and liberal society found there. The jobs these immigrants found, however, were often harsh. Irish immigrant women generally worked as domestics in the homes of wealthier Americans or they toiled in the textile mills. In Wisconsin, farm work and the teaching professions were more likely occupations than mill work. Despite this slight deviation from the national norm, Wisconsin did not lack for women in what is regarded as the blue-collar labor force. One of the great labor organizers and reformers—not to mention suffragists—of the early twentieth century was Maude McCreery, born in Wauwatosa in 1883 and of Irish extraction. McCreery's accomplishments indicate that these Irish women in Wisconsin had a level of independence often unachievable in Ireland.

The Irish immigrants of the nineteenth century tended to choose urban locations over rural, settling in the large cities of the East Coast like Boston, Philadelphia, and New York, and, as the century wore on, Chicago and other large cities of the Midwest. Newly arriving immigrants in turn would also move to the city to seek out fellow countrymen. About 85 percent of Irish American Catholics worked in industry or in the transportation sector (usually the railroad), and only 15 percent were engaged in farming. This is odd considering the agricultural nature of their life back in Ireland. But despite their rural lifestyle in Ireland, many of the Irish were not well versed in modern farming techniques and they had little experience in managing their own farms. They may have had strong bonds to the land, but Irish peasants were among the most inefficient farmers in Europe. Irish immigrants also moved to urban areas because they wished to be near the Catholic Church and its clergy and these were easier to find in a city than in the country or in certain cities in the South. Many of the earliest Irish Catholic immigrants who settled in the South and in Appalachia eventually lost their religion because the Catholic Church was not prevalent in those regions.

In the early 1840s Daniel O'Connell (1775–1847) began to organize mass meetings to push for the repeal of the repressive Act of Union between Ireland and Great Britain, using the same tactics he had used in the Catholic Emancipation campaign decades earlier. O'Connell's Repeal Association even had a branch in Milwaukee, which sent £1,219 to Ireland. Although the famine prevented O'Connell from achieving his goal, he did succeed in politicizing the Irish masses.

WHS Name File

Henry S. Baird (1800–1875), a Dublin native, arrived in the midwest in 1822 and moved to Green Bay in 1824. He was the first person to practice law in what would become the State of Wisconsin. A political career followed, which included serving as attorney general of the territory, president of the first territorial council, delegate to the Wisconsin Constitutional Convention, and mayor of Green Bay.

PH 60

The Irish and General Emigration Land Agency Office opened in Milwaukee in 1849, and various services like the Travellers' Home appeared at that time as well, allowing Irish immigrants who were escaping the famine a new home and hope.

Above: In 1860, just prior to the outbreak of war, city leadership in Milwaukee included numerous men originally from Ireland. Many were on board the *Lady Elgin* when it sank returning from Chicago. One can only guess how the city would have developed had so many of its Irish leaders not gone down in Lake Michigan.

Left: R. J. O. McGowan Civil War portrait, Berlin.

The 17th Wisconsin Regimental veterans flag listing the various battles the men who cried out in Irish, *Faugh a ballagh!* (Clear the way!), in the face of so many bloody battles.

In 1889, nearly a quarter century after the war, members of the 17th Wisconsin reunited in Milwaukee.

TO WISCONSIN

On, Wisconsin! On, Wisconsin!
Grand old badger state!
We, thy loyal sons and daughters,
Hail thee, good and great.
On, Wisconsin! On, Wisconsin!
Champion of the right,
"Forward," our motto
God will give thee might!"

"On, Wisconsin!" by Charles D. Rosa
and J. S. Hubbard

Why Wisconsin? Before exploring some specific reasons, let us reflect back on why most Irish immigrants decided to settle in the cities of the East Coast. They enjoyed the camaraderie and familiarity of being surrounded by their fellow countrymen. Agricultural and small town life were more isolating, and although the immigrants had lived in these types of communities in Ireland, the distances between friends and relatives there was much shorter than it was in America. Remember that most Irish people never traveled out of their home county and the entire country was only a little larger than the combined size of Indiana and Ohio. It took a special outlook to decide to break free from this familiarity and settle in territory that was oftentimes uncharted. An entrepreneurial spirit and a willingness to take chances were sometimes necessary prerequisites to making the trek westward—first to the United States and then to areas like Wisconsin. The Irish emigrant had to break free of the "passive exile" mold and embrace a more active role in his or her destiny.

It may not be entirely accurate to say that the Irish in Wisconsin often had these independent and entrepreneurial traits in more abundance than the Irish who decided to stay in the big cities of the East, because there are many interdependent factors that led to differences in social and economic success. These can range from the relative resources among migrant groups, to regional socioeconomic groups, to trends in family dynamics that did not tolerate greater success of one generation over another. However, it is true—as Lawrence McCaffrey, a historian of

Irish America, writes—that, "Newly arrived immigrants in the Midwest were more likely to succeed than third or fourth generation Irish Catholics in Boston." For whatever reason, Midwestern Irish Americans tended to be more confident and competitive within American society than their Eastern brethren. Edmund Greany's story is typical of many Irish immigrants who chose Wisconsin. He came to America in 1848, settled in New York and worked for the Hudson River Railroad. Edmund came over with his brother and they later brought their wives. Perhaps the men would have been content to stay in New York where Edmund had a decent job, but Edmund's sister-in-law, "who could always see bright things in the distance," wanted to go west to Iowa or Michigan, and purchase cheap land. They eventually moved to Wisconsin and settled along the Grant River near Slabtown in Grant County (located near present-day Beetown Township).

An Irish immigrant in New York would have heard about cheap land and good opportunities in Wisconsin because of the young state's concerted efforts (and prior to that the territorial government) to advertise Wisconsin as an attractive choice for the newly arrived immigrant. As early as the 1840s, articles appeared in Eastern newspapers urging Irish immigrants to move to Wisconsin. One advertisement that appeared claimed "Fifty years labor in New England or twenty years' toil in Ohio are not equal in their result to five industrious years in Wisconsin." Wisconsin also produced pamphlets, emigrant guides, and state histories that extolled the virtues of the state. The Wisconsin State Emigrant Agency opened in 1852 in New York and provided information to immigrants from many European countries. Further legislation allowed for a traveling agent to move between New York and Wisconsin, "to see that correct representations be made in eastern papers of our Wisconsin's great natural resources, advantages, and privileges, and brilliant prospects for the future; and to use every honorable means in his power to induce emigrants to come to this state." Unfortunately these legislative efforts were eventually ended because of pressure from Nativists, "Yankees" who sought the same benefits for themselves. Perhaps John Solon and his family were influenced by the state's efforts at promotion. John wrote, "When leaving Ireland (his father) had decided to go to Chicago and settle somewhere in Illinois, but about this time there was a boom for Wisconsin and after a couple of weeks . . . we took passage for Milwaukee."

Irish groups too made a concerted effort to settle Irish immigrants in
rural areas. Organizations like the Catholic Emigration Society, the Irish
National Emigration Society, and the Irish Pioneer Emigration Fund, all
of which had first attempted to improve the lot of Irish immigrants by
pushing for better conditions on the "coffin ships" and preventing Irish
people from being defrauded, later offered incentives for urban dwellers
to settle in rural areas. These efforts often faltered, though, because the
Irish leaders of the Catholic Church were reluctant to give their blessing
to a plan that might put Irish Catholics out of the reach of priest and
parish. In the late nineteenth century, by the time these programs had
started to gain what little momentum they were to achieve, Wisconsin
was targeting Germans and Norwegians to settle the land. In 1895 the
Catholic Sentinel of Chippewa Falls ran an editorial complaining about
the State Board of Immigration and its lack of focus on the Irish:

> We fail to see the name of a man on (the governor's) list from that
> nation which gave America the greatest number of immigrants,
> and whose blood and brain and muscle are found in two-thirds of
> all the masterminds and sturdy workers of the Union. That nation
> whose lusty sons dug our canals, built our railroads and manned our
> vessels, whose influence made Boston, New York and Chicago what
> they are, has no representative on Governor Upham's immigrant
> commission. No Irish need apply to him for place or position. He
> wants none but Norwegians to people the houseless wilds of Mara-
> thon and Marshfield.

By the time this editorial was written, some historians claim, the Irish flavor of Wisconsin was fading fast.

One of the most important reasons Irish immigrants chose to come
to Wisconsin was the recommendations they received from family and
friends who lived here. All that was needed, in some instances, was one
Irish family or a couple of Irishmen to bring about an influx of friends
and family. In Mount Hope Township (popularly known as Irish Ridge)
in Grant County, one unnamed Irish immigrant convinced his former
neighbors from Vermont to join him in Wisconsin. In this way, one person could influence others who, in turn, brought even more Irish pioneers, producing a steady flow of new settlers. William Shea knew he was
headed to Fond du Lac before he left Ireland. He had an uncle Joe who

lived in Osceola. William wrote about sending for his siblings: "I sent for George, George sent for Joe, Joe sent for Mike. My sister Bridget, who is married to Mike Sullivan and lives in Milwaukee, came here when she was about twenty. The folks paid her way over here, because she was going to marry someone over there they didn't like, so they sent her to America."

Sometimes Irish settlers were pointed in the direction of Wisconsin by chance. Bryan, Terrence, and Dennis O'Loghlin immigrated to America during the famine and came from one of the worst hit areas of the country—the Burren in Co. Clare. Like the Solons, they originally planned on settling in Illinois; however according to the O'Loghlins, "A Mr. Snowbrook, whom they met on the boat after leaving Buffalo, said to them, 'Why go to Illinois? The people there are suffering with fever and ague. The drinking water is bad. Why not go to Wisconsin where it is healthy and they have the best drinking water in the world.'" Dennis O'Loghlin's experience provides an example of how Wisconsin's reputation drew immigrants and also hints at one of the concerns of settling in rural areas:

> We traveled through Albany, Buffalo, Detroit, Macanaw and Milwaukee from thence to Sheboygan in the state of Wisconsin, where we have been directed by experienced travelers who state this locality to be the most healthy and richest part of America, although thinly settled yet. We intend to look out for a farm which we hope can be had without much trouble. The only great disadvantage we feel here is the want of a Catholic clergyman.

As to where in Wisconsin people would settle once they arrived there, that too was often the result of chance. John Solon recalled: "While walking the streets of Milwaukee one day (his father) happened to meet a fellow Irishman by the name of Patrick Fitzgerald who was after buying 80 acres of government land in the town of Shields, Dodge County, and had (procured) another 80. (Father) bought cheap without seeing or knowing what he was getting, but it happened to be all right and as good as the 80 Fitzgerald had."

These individual examples are helpful in explaining why some immigrants settled in Wisconsin. But we have yet to touch on one of the main reasons Wisconsin's first Irish settlers came here.

LIVELIHOODS

In eighteen hundred and forty-one
My corduroy breeches I put on
My corduroy breeches I put on
To work upon the railway, the railway
I'm weary of the railway
Poor Paddy works on the railway
"Paddy Works on the Railway," Traditional

If one were to look at a map of foreign-born Irish in the state of Wisconsin in both 1850 and 1860, one would notice a concentration in places like Milwaukee, Fond du Lac, and later, Madison, but there is also a concentration in the southwest corner of the state, particularly in Lafayette and Iowa counties. Recent studies indicate that in the year 2000 the two most Irish cities or towns in Wisconsin were found in Lafayette County: Darlington (25 percent claim Irish heritage) and Shullsburg (24 percent). The Irish—like two other ethnic groups from the British Isles, the Welsh and the Cornish—came to this area to work in the lead mines. The lead mining region of Wisconsin was composed of the present counties of Grant, Iowa, Lafayette, and the western edge of Dane and Green Counties. At their peak performance, in 1847, these mines of southwestern Wisconsin (and northwestern Illinois) were producing 85 percent of the world's lead. These miners came early to Wisconsin, mostly preceding the great wave of famine immigrants. The 1836 territorial census shows that at least one-tenth of the names of the approximately 1,000 heads of families listed for Iowa County were Irish. As the economy of the region transitioned to farming in the 1850s, many of these miners moved into agriculture, while others left the state for different jobs and more adventure.

One natural choice for some of these former miners may have been the move into the boom business of the mid- to late nineteenth century—the railroads. Between 1850 and 1860 railroads had begun to penetrate the interior of the state, and by 1900 they had spread their iron tentacles across the entire state. In the 1850s and 1860s, those towns and cities with the highest concentrations of Irish born people were often those places where the railroad was being built. The trains brought both new immigrants to an area and the Irish transportation workers constructing the railroads. In 1859, Waukesha County, the first county in Wisconsin to see real railroad development, ranked first among Wisconsin counties in Irish born inhabitants. The city of Whitewater grew rapidly after the railroad extended from Waukesha to Janesville. Rock County saw its Irish population increase by 264 percent after the trains came. Some of this increase was, as indicated, due to easier accessibility to these towns, but most was due to the workers who settled there during the process of working the rails. These laborers tended to move west with the railway, making the great influx of Irish inhabitants in many Wisconsin towns temporary. Some stayed in Wisconsin but moved to the bigger cities to find work or they moved to small towns and villages and bought farms. For example, when railroad failures in 1857 suspended work on the Superior and Bayfield lines in Hudson, St. Croix County, a colony of laborers settled in the countryside permanently and helped build that county's reputation as a haven for the Irish.

Another aspect of Wisconsin's infrastructure that the Irish contributed to was the canals, locks, and dams that went into the Fox and Wisconsin River improvements. The hard labor needed for this vast engineering project was often supplied by Irish workers. One Irish settler wrote in 1852, of the booming area around Portage:

> Having got beyond the boundary of civilization in the Far West, I send you a hurried scrap. I will first try your geographical knowledge. . . . You may ransack all the charts, maps, atlases, and geographies in Boston, and not be able to find Goudgeville. . . . About two years ago a canal was commenced here at Fort Winnebago to join the Fox and Wisconsin rivers. At the head of this canal a town sprang up in a few days, with the rapidity of a mushroom. It being in the Indian reserve, and the lands not of course in market, every one claimed a lot for himself, built on it, and lives on it without having paid the government a cent. They have changed its name from Goudgeville to Portage City. It bids fair to be a place of considerable importance, being situated at the junction of the Fox and Wisconsin Rivers, the navigation of both will soon be completed. Boats can run from the Mississippi up the Wisconsin River to this place, and will shortly be able to pass down the Fox River to Lake Winnebago, thence to Green Bay, and into the great Western Lakes. . . . It is rather far north, winter sets in early, and spring is long in making its appearance.

Like the railroad workers, many of these men moved on from Wisconsin after their work was finished; however, a great many stayed on and helped foster those Irish settlements in the center of the state up to Green Bay.

Like their counterparts on the East Coast, the Irish of Wisconsin were also drawn to the larger cities. In 1850, the Irish made up 15 percent of Milwaukee's population. The southern section of the city east of the Milwaukee River became Irish territory. The Third Ward—or the "Bloody Third" because of its raucous nature—was 60 percent Irish in the 1850s and 1860s. Similarly, over half of the Irish residents in Dane County lived in Madison and its surrounding townships of Fitchburg, Dunn, Cottage Grove, and Westport. In Madison, they settled in the area southwest of the capital—coincidently also termed the "Bloody" or "Fighting Fourth" Ward. Most of the Irish in the cities were manual laborers. Irish women worked as housewives and domestics, and in dressmaking, millinery, laundering, teaching, and nursing. Working as a manual laborer was difficult but it provided a family with the money to ensure better opportunities for the next generation.

Working in the meat packing industry gave one family the business experience and work ethic necessary for great success. The Cudahy brothers' family left Callan, Co. Kilkenny, in 1849 because of the Famine and settled in Milwaukee. Michael, Patrick Jr., John, and Edward, were all employed in the hard work of meatpacking. Rising through the ranks of employees with hard work and ingenuity, the brothers soon made a name for themselves. John and Patrick Jr. formed the Cudahy Brothers Packing Company in Milwaukee in 1888, and in 1890, Michael and Edward started the Cudahy Packing Company based out of Chicago and Omaha. Both businesses were very successful and made the Cudahys millionaires. The family's wealth and success led to influence outside of the meatpacking industry. For example, Patrick's son John C. Cudahy went on to become U.S. ambassador to Poland, Ireland, and Belgium in the 1930s and 1940s. The town of Cudahy, south of Milwaukee, developed around one of the packing plants and a statue of the town's founding father, Patrick Cudahy, stands as a testament to the hard work and perseverance of the Irish in Wisconsin.

Patrick Cudahy was the son of an Irish immigrant and his success shows that the second- and third- generation Irish in America were better able to take advantage of the opportunities provided by the United

States than their parents. Their mothers and fathers faced discrimination, lack of certain skills, and often a language barrier that made it difficult to do anything other than manual labor or farm work. Due to their
parents' and grandparents' hard work, the following generations were
able to receive the education necessary to join the professions. For both
Irish women and men, teaching became a popular career choice. In the
nineteenth century, teaching was one of the few professions open to
women, and Irish women took full advantage of the opportunity to edu-
cate the youth of their communities. One extended family in the St.
Croix valley, the Reardons and Stapletons, sent almost all their daughters
and quite a few of their sons to the teaching profession. The family provided a steady stream of students for the State Normal School in River
Falls (now the University of Wisconsin–River Falls). One member of the
extended family, J. D. O'Keefe, ran as the Republican candidate for
County Superintendent of Schools for St. Croix and won—he gained a
surprising 51 of 56 votes in the heavily Democratic and heavily Irish
township of Erin Prairie. Apparently ethnic considerations sometimes
overrode political convictions.

In 1923 D. J. Hemlock, an attorney, presented a paper on the promi-
nent members of the Irish community in Waukesha County, to a local historical society. For the reader unfamiliar with the Irish social scene of
Waukesha in the 1920s, his essay soon bogs down in a list of unpro-
nounceable Gaelic names. Hemlock's purpose in presenting this material,
however, is quite interesting. "Many names have been left unmentioned
of Irish lineage, men and women of standing in industry, education,
valor," he wrote, "but enough has been said to show that Bridget has left
the kitchen and Patrick has left the ditch and have gone to higher walks
in life, the women as well as the men have gone into business, the men
and women have gone into the practice of law and medicine." For many
Americans of Irish heritage it was important to show that they had inte-
grated successfully into American society, and that the old stereotypes no
longer held true.

The Irish in Wisconsin also made a solid contribution to the legal
profession. The most famous jurist of Irish extraction was Edward G.
Ryan, born in Ireland in 1810. He moved to Wisconsin after earning his
legal and political pedigree in the hard-knock world of New York's Tammany Hall. He was elected to Wisconsin's Constitutional Convention in
1846 and played a major role during his tenure there. In particular, he

made a name for himself in state politics as author of the anti-bank article that led to the defeat of the 1846 Constitution. As a lifetime Democrat, his political fortunes declined as the Civil War approached and Wisconsin became a predominantly Republican state. During the Civil War he was vocal in his opposition to President Lincoln's war policies and became a leader of the Copperhead wing of the Democratic Party. In 1874, the Democrats briefly gained political control of the state and Ryan was appointed as Chief Justice of the Wisconsin Supreme Court, where he remained for six years until his death in 1880. His work in those years established him as one of the great American state court justices of the nineteenth century.

One final example should be mentioned because it again illustrates the type of person who chose to come to Wisconsin. John Gregory of Rathskea, Co. Kerry, was an accomplished man in Ireland. He was an educator who held the following positions: Master of the English, Mathematical and Mercantile Departments of the Diocesan School of Cork; Professor in the endowed school at Kilrush; Head Master at Ennis Academy; and President of the College of Civil Engineering, Mining and Agriculture in Dublin. He published works in Ireland on astronomy, mathematics, and engineering, and even the invention of a "steam carriage for the common roads." In 1849 he immigrated to America and moved to Milwaukee in 1850. In 1855 he published *The Industrial Resources of Wisconsin*, a book where he combined descriptions of these inventions and industrial successes in Ireland and England, with the potential successes Wisconsin had to offer with its diverse natural resources and prime location on the North American continent. The book, published in two volumes and in two different editions played no small role in attracting industry to the state. He also served as secretary of the Irish National Emigration Society.

RURAL LIFE

It's hard to be forced from the lands that we live in,
Our houses and farms obliged for to sell,
And to wander alone amongst Indians and strangers
To find some sweet spot where our children might dwell.
I've got a wee lassie I fain would take with me,
Her dwelling at present lies in County Down,
It would break my sad heart for to leave her behind me,
We will both roam together the wide world around.
So come away, Bessie, my own blue-eyed lassie,
Bid farewell to your mother and then come with me,
I'll do my endeavor to keep your mind cheery
Till we reach the green fields of Americay.

"The Green Fields of Americay, " Traditional

The type of personality needed to escape the closely-knit Irish communities of the East Coast, often contained the character traits found in the Wisconsin Irish who worked the land. The Irish saw themselves as exiles from their native land and many knew enough about familial, local and/or national history to know that their land was now owned by the English. To be sure, even if the British had never come, many of these people would not have owned land, but it was their perception that they were kicked off land that rightfully belonged to them. And perception is powerful. Ownership of land became an important goal for the Irish immigrant for economic and symbolic reasons. Land in America was abundant and the government made it available for relatively low sums of money.

In Wisconsin after 1850, the number of Irish engaged in agricultural work was greater than that in any other industry. Many of the miners of the southwest part of the state took up farming when mine work slowed and then stopped. The same can be said of railroad workers and the "navvies" who dug the canals and trenches for the Fox River improvements. In Winnebago, Outagamie, Brown, and Marquette Counties, most of the Irish were farmers, and many of those had come to the area because of the Fox River improvements. Many Irish people working as laborers in the towns and cities of Wisconsin saved enough money to allow themselves or their offspring to buy farmland. However, a significant percentage of the Irish in Wisconsin who were engaged in agriculture came to the state specifically to farm and thus settled upon the land right after moving.

William Shea was lucky enough to have a support group in Osceola and Fond du Lac, but he still had to work in order to save money to purchase land. He started out as a laborer for farmers who were also of Irish background. At one job, during the 1880s, he was hired on for $140 a year; that rate was later raised to $155. He budgeted for a savings of $100 for a land purchase, $20 to send to his "folk" in Ireland, and $20 for expenses for the upcoming year. Shea's remittance home eventually paid for his siblings' passage to America, and he was eventually able to buy the land he wanted and build a farm on it. He was to remain a farmer for forty years. It would be difficult to say that Mr. Shea ever retired. He wrote, "A couple of days after celebrating my 86th birthday, I earned $11.50 for a day's work."

William Shea was a native Irish speaker so that was the language he was most familiar with when he came to this country. Language was at the center of an amusing anecdote he recalled about trying to find the home of his Uncle Joe Shea. He first asked two men mixing mortar how to get to his Uncle Joe's and they replied to him in a strange language that he later realized must have been German. Then he came across some teenage girls: "When I asked them the way to Uncle Joe's, they started making fun of me, and I told them in Irish they could kiss my ass and one girl answers back in Irish and said, 'I don't have to.'" His encounter with Irish speakers in Fond du Lac County is intriguing. The Irish language actually survived longer in remote and rural areas than it did in the cities. In Wisconsin, there were many townships and villages that, because of their rural isolation, retained the language and culture of Ireland largely unadulterated. These towns often bore names that hint at their Irish character. There is Erin Prairie in St. Croix County, Erin Township in Washington County, Westport (named after the town in Co. Mayo, Ireland, from where most of its settlers came) in Dane County, and Emmet and Shields (named after famous Irish) in Dodge County. Other Irish agricultural towns include: Monches (originally called O'Connellsville after the great Irish statesman) in Waukesha County, Meemes in Manitowoc County, Osceola and Eden in Fond du Lac County, and oddly named El Paso in Pierce County.

Grace McDonald, who was the first historian of the Irish in Wisconsin, wrote of a township in Sauk County commenting, "Loreto was one of those Irish agricultural communities of successful farmers who remained relatively shut off from the rest of the world clinging to their Irish traditions and customs." Because they were, in many ways, isolated from outside influences, these communities were able to preserve Irish traditions at a level unknown in more populated cities. In these close-knit communities, the evening's entertainment often centered around visiting neighbors where they would tell humorous tales and ghost stories and sing songs—a simple custom but one that was traditionally Irish. Weddings, baptisms, and funerals (and the accompanying wake) were all held in the traditional Irish way. Keeners, for example, sang dirges and lamentations for the deceased at many Irish funerals in Wisconsin. These keeners were female and they often expressed great drama and emotion while bewailing the dead. In Ireland the family of the deceased hired keeners for the funeral if that family did not have one among their members. Clergy tried to stamp out keening, which they considered unseemly, during the Devotional Revolution, and succeeded. However, in the small towns of Wisconsin, this practice survived. In 1944, historian Fred L. Holmes encountered a man from Erin Prairie who bemoaned the recent dearth of some of these traditional practices:

> There hasn't been a real wake here for ten years. Instead, two or three friends are designated to sit with the dead through the nights before burial. At least a part of the old custom has been retained. And it is at least twenty-five years since an Irish keener has appeared at any of our funerals. Customs may disappear but still a man would be a poor judge who would mistake an Irishman from Erin Prairie for any other nationality.

Despite their gradual disappearance, these old customs still lasted a long time—longer than they survived in much of Ireland—and the old ways still resonate with today's Irish in Wisconsin who celebrate the life of a deceased friend or family member with an "Irish wake."

William Shea provided a good comparison between his life in Wisconsin and the life he had in Ireland. After he settled down with a wife and had two children, William returned to the land of his birth twenty-five years after he left. His parents did not eat with them, "The reason was they were too shy to have Miles and Hannah (William's children) see how they ate. They would fry the fish and throw them right on the bare table and everybody reached in and grabbed. Potatoes were boiled in a big iron kettle, skins and all, about a bushel at a time and spread on the table." He described the house where he was born as being built of mud and standing 20' x 60'. The diet in the part of Ireland where he was raised consisted mainly of potatoes and sour milk (known in Ireland as bonnyclabber), and "our meat for Christmas dinner and for Easter was pig's head." As for dress, William wrote, "Women never wore shoes in the week and children never wore shoes at all until they were from ten to twelve years old." Life in a new country was certainly difficult, but people like William Shea realized that America provided opportunities and comforts not available in Ireland. Shea was able to buy his own farm and attain the comforts associated with a modern industrial society.

Irish immigrants wrote paeans to their motherland, and they felt exiled by an alien force from the country they loved. However, they also often realized the great bounty this new land provided for them. The following is taken from a letter written by Dennis O'Loghlin to his brother Laurence at the time of the famine. The letter shows the excitement that came with settling in a new land, along with the reasons he considered Wisconsin such a great place for a farmer to live:

> The City of Fond du Lac calls to me mind the state of Carthage when Æneas entered it. All persons busy about building. Some in this street, some in that street. All cluttering about business and buildings. . . . But I am told by some Irishmen from Leinster that the herbiage [in Fond du Lac County] is so sweet that Ireland could not fatten a cow or a bullock faster or better than those woods. . . . This Prairie can never be exhausted by cropping it with corn or oats. . . . The house we have got on this land is built of good solid oak logs 26 by 20 by 11 feet, his [brother Terrence] with a large cellar and upper chambers.
>
> You seem anxious to know the manners and customs of our neighbors the Dutch [German]. They are all Catholics. Stout rough built robust cheery pleasant fellows. O' Laurence *the women* are far below the men in shape and beauty. The best about the shape and figure of Norry Grady but hardly so tall. Our Priest is Dutch and a very zealous man he is. The Yankees are intricketable [intractable] dealers in this country.

No fairs held in this state as stock is as yet scarce but jobbers take in stock from Indiana and Illinois.

Now Dear brother you want my decided opinion as to a choice of both countries. . . . But if I were now back in Ireland and to be offered Glendine for one half your rent and that for ninety nine [years], I would rather live on 80 acres of Wisconsin. I do expect to live twice better and more comfortable than you can, every man eats meat twice or three times a day and three sorts of bread too here. The only difference that is, is that you must be your own work-man as to the soil, after a few plowings one horse is sufficient to work, a man need not work hard.

The last part of Dennis's letter could be written off as an exaggeration along the lines of "the streets are paved with gold" except that it was more or less true.

POLITICAL LIFE

When boyhood's fire was in my blood
I read of ancient freemen,
For Greece and Rome who bravely stood,
Three hundred men and three men;
And then I prayed I yet might see
Our fetters rent in twain,
And Ireland, long a province, be
A Nation once again!

"A Nation Once Again, " by Thomas Davis

It did not take long for Irish immigrants and their progeny to acclimate to American politics. The Irish became a force in politics soon after they began arriving in large numbers. Their influence was obviously most felt in those areas of the country where they made up a significant percent-age of the population. However, their influence did not arise simply out of their numbers. Other ethnic groups, like the Germans, also came to the United States in great numbers in the mid- to late nineteenth century, but these groups did not have the impact on American politics that the

Irish had. By the twentieth century, the Irish had gained control in most major American cities, including New York, Chicago, Boston, and San Francisco. These Irish politicians and the political machines they led have often been criticized for their harmful effects on the morality of American politics. New York's Tammany Hall, for example, was notorious for its graft.

Yet the Irish did not corrupt a system that was pure nor did they forever taint the political systems of American cities. The Anglo-Americans who ran these cities prior to the Irish gaining influence were only too willing to use graft and corruption to hold onto power, and they often used the Irish immigrants and their votes to retain their seats. Most Irish politicians, however, did not let idealism stand in the way of accomplishing real reform that benefited the urban poor and other ethnic groups. Historian Lawrence McCaffrey wrote of the accomplishment of Irish-American politicians, "While adjusting other Catholic ethnics to America (by showing them the ropes of political life) and propelling a reluctant nation along the road to economically and socially interventionist government, Irish Catholic politicians were quietly achieving a successful social revolution in the status and condition of their own people."

How were the Irish able to achieve their political successes in such a relatively short period of time? The answer lies in the burgeoning nationalist movement in Ireland. Earlier it was mentioned that before and during the famine, Irish immigrants were likely to view themselves as Kerrymen or Corkmen rather than Irishmen. However, changes in national identity were also occurring during this period. Although, to this day, Irish people still identify strongly with their hometown or county, the nineteenth century was a period when people in Ireland began to identify themselves as Irish. Daniel O'Connell greatly contributed to this development. A successful Catholic lawyer from Kerry, O'Connell launched the greatest extra-parliamentary movement ever seen in the British Isles. By the early nineteenth century many of the Penal Laws had been rescinded, but Catholics still did not have the right to sit in Parliament because to do so they had to take an oath antithetical to their beliefs. O'Connell founded the Catholic Association in 1823 for the purpose of winning basic political rights for Roman Catholics. The Catholic Association was a mass movement that allowed for participation across class boundaries. O'Connell charged a "rent," or a fee, that could be as little as a penny a month—an amount even a poor peasant could afford. In this way, he was able to rally Irish Catholics around a single cause and showed what numbers and determination could accomplish. Catholic Emancipation was granted in 1828. This event was a landmark in the history of mass political movements and it led inexorably to the political awakening of the Irish nation.

After this success, O'Connell moved on to the bigger challenge of repealing the Act of Union between Ireland and Great Britain. In the early 1840s, O'Connell began to organize mass meetings to push for repeal. He used the same tactics he had used in the Catholic Emancipation campaign. At Tara (the traditional seat of the ancient Irish kingdom located in Co. Meath) in 1843, approximately one million people took part in one of these "monster" meetings; the sheer numbers attending these events attracted the attention of the British government. O'Connell's Repeal Association even had a branch in Milwaukee and it was able to send £1,219 to O'Connell's Association in Ireland. The famine, combined with other factors, took the steam out of the repeal movement and it never achieved its goals; however, O'Connell did succeed in politicizing the Irish masses.

This political awareness worked in tandem with a rapidly improving literacy rate in Ireland. By 1900 the literacy rate was higher than in the United States. The Irish people were able to read nationalist newspapers like *The Nation* and *The Freeman's Journal*, both of which emphasized the Irish people's need to take control of their destiny and obtain their own government. When Irish immigrants arrived on American shores, most had the advantage of not only speaking English, but also knowing how participatory democracy was supposed to function—an advantage not available to many other immigrant groups.

In Wisconsin, the Irish had an almost immediate impact on politics. Because Wisconsin became a state in 1848, its political institutions and parties were not in the hands of entrenched groups when the first waves of Irish immigrants came to the area. In New York and Boston, the Irish had to work with and then unseat the Anglo power structure that had held sway since the seventeenth century. In Wisconsin, this level playing field did not translate into Irish control of state politics, but it did mean that the Irish played a formidable role in the formation of the state's political system.

The Irish and German immigrants in Wisconsin territory and their later influx into the state bulked up the ranks of the Democratic Party.

The Irish, even more than the Germans, were staunch supporters of the Democrats. This allegiance was often forged in the cities of the East Coast, where the Democrats were the party of the immigrants. The Whigs, on the other hand, had a strong nativist contingent. In Wisconsin territory, the Democrats pushed for a liberal suffrage that would allow foreigners the right to vote on statehood questions and elect delegates to the constitutional convention, but, at the same time, limited the vote to white male inhabitants over twenty-one years of age who had resided in the territory for three months. That residency requirement was amended in 1845 to six months and the prospective voter had to declare his intention to become a citizen if he was not already naturalized. These measures were passed by Democratic legislatures and liberal suffrage was later embodied in the state constitution by a Democratic controlled convention. The Irish and Germans became closely tied to the Democrats because of their support for these voting concessions, but the Democrats, in turn, also relied on Irish and German support to retain power in the first state elections.

The Irish were well aware of their political clout. One editorial in a Catholic newspaper in Milwaukee urged "sons of 'Erin's Green Isle,' to lose not one minute, but go and declare their intentions to become citizens of these United States, and then, according to law, they will be entitled to vote at the coming struggle at the next town meeting, and for delegates to form a state constitution." Seven Irishmen were elected to the first constitutional convention and five to the second. Although they complained that they were discriminated against in caucus and rejected for office, they did receive perks commensurate with their influence. In the years between 1848 and 1853, school fund loans distributed for the establishment of local schools granted largely as political favors. The Irish, who made up about 7 percent of the population, received 13.5 percent of the loans granted, while the Germans, who made up 12.5 percent of the population, received only 2.3 percent of the loans. A historian of the period remarked upon the political savvy of the Irish:

> It is well known that the Germans of this early period were politically quiescent and tractable; they were not yet trained to active participation in politics and, in a word, did not 'count' politically. With the Irish the case was exactly reversed. They were so alert, vigorous, and insistent, so class conscious withal, that it was worthwhile for politicians to take special pains to conciliate their support.

Political lessons learned in Ireland and in the cities of the East Coast produced positive results in Wisconsin.

Throughout the nineteenth century there were two main factors that shaped the Irish political agenda—Irish nationalism and Roman Catholicism. A political issue that could be spun to be pro-Ireland or anti-Britain was usually a sure vote-getter. For example, the majority Democratic legislature passed a joint resolution in 1852 expressing sympathy with the Irish patriots John Mitchell, William Smith O'Brien, and T. Francis Meagher. These men were in prison in Great Britain for their role in a nationalist revolt in Ireland in 1848. (Mitchell later escaped to America). The resolution called for their release and their return to their homeland or the United States, and was a blatant attempt to curry favor with the Irish. The Whig governor, Leonard J. Farwell, vetoed the resolution but expressed sympathy with its objective. Even though the Irish were overwhelmingly Democrats, the Whigs and Republicans could not disregard their vote. For example, as Grace McDonald states in *The History of the Irish in Wisconsin*, "Whig papers, especially in Irish communities, made overtures to the Irish-born inhabitants on the grounds that Franklin Pierce (a Democrat) opposed a protective tariff, while all great Irish leaders favored it as a means of cutting into English profits on American trade." More often than not, however, these tactics by the Whigs and Republicans won only minimal and/or temporary support from Irish voters. There were Wisconsin Irish who voted with the Whigs and Republicans, but the stain of nativism clung to these parties too much for them to ever receive a great deal of Irish support.

Occasionally there were Irishmen like Alexander McGowan, who emigrated from County Down. He was a disciple of John Mitchell and a diehard Irish nationalist. Although he began his life in America as a Democrat, he switched to the Republican Party because of the slavery issue. According to family records housed at the Wisconsin Historical Society,"[H]is ideas of liberty were not of that narrow class which asked for the freedom of his own friends and countrymen only, but for the liberation of the world's captives be they black or white." Alexander's son, Robert, fought in the Civil War in the 33rd and 47th Regiments of the Wisconsin Volunteer Infantry and obtained the rank of captain. His father, a strong supporter of the Republicans, the Union, and the freedom of others must have been proud.

SERVING THE UNION

When we got home at night, boys, the divil a bite we'd ate,
We'd sit up and drink a sup of whisky strong and nate
Then we'd all march home together as slippery as lard,
The solid men would all fall in and march with the Mulligan Guard

"The Mulligan Guards," by Edward Harrington and David Braham

Irishmen did not let their political allegiance stop them from volunteering in great numbers in Wisconsin. They were among the first in the state to enter the Union army. The one-hundred-man Montgomery Guards of Milwaukee, led by captain J. O'Rourke, formed part of the famed Iron Brigade (the 6th Wisconsin Volunteer Infantry). James "Mickey" Sullivan, also of the 6th Wisconsin, was the only man in his regiment to formally enlist on three separate occasions. One comrade claimed, "A hundred men wore the star of generals who did not dare or do as much in the war as J. P. Sullivan." He later recorded his recollections in a regular column for the *Milwaukee Sunday Telegraph;* these recollections were later edited into a book that provides valuable insight into the life of a Wisconsin soldier during the Civil War, *An Irishman in the Iron Brigade: The Civil War Memoirs of James P. Sullivan, Sergt., Company K, 6th Wisconsin Volunteers.* A Wisconsin Irish regiment, the 17th, was formed in the spring of 1862 and contained such colorful company names as the Mulligan Guards of Kenosha, the Peep O'Day Boys of Racine, and the Emmett Guards of Dodge. Their Irishness was evident at the battle of Corinth, where the men of the 17th led a bayonet charge with the Gaelic battle cry *Faugh a Ballagh!* ("Clear the Way!"). The Irish in the Union Army were even able to turn the Civil War into an Irish nationalist action in part because of significant British support for the Confederacy. Furthermore, many looked upon the war as excellent training for future efforts to win Irish freedom.

The Civil War had an interesting impact on Irish American politics in Wisconsin. According to the historian Grace McDonald, "The formation of the Irish regiment served to stimulate a group consciousness among the Irishmen of the state which was not existent prior to this time. . . . As a result the Irish of the state became more politically self-conscious, thus precipitating a more united action on their part when the

Fenian movement roused their Irish ire against England and their political ire against those who stood in the way of their success." Similar to the way in which Irish immigrants were forced by American realities to see themselves as Irishmen rather than Corkmen or Kerrymen, the Civil War bolstered Irish nationalism among Wisconsin veterans and brought home the importance of acting together statewide as a political force. Unfortunately for their statewide political ambitions, the Democrats were the minority party in Wisconsin for most of the period after the Civil War.

But then the Fenian movement arrived and provided an outlet for Irish political ambitions. The Fenian Brotherhood was an Irish nationalist group formed in the United States. Its objective was to overthrow British rule in Ireland. With that goal, when the Civil War ended in 1865, the Fenians decided that the time was right for an invasion of Canada. By invading part of the British Empire the Fenians, in a not very well-thought out plan, hoped to provoke a British crisis that would lead to warfare and eventual freedom for Ireland. Anti-British sentiment was high, and the Irish in America had just received invaluable training in warfare. But the invasion was a fiasco, partly because the Fenian leadership split over the logistics of the invasion. The Wisconsin Fenians, with over six thousand members, reflected the confusion and divisions on the national level. However, the U.S. government's response to the feeble invasion—arresting Fenian leaders and ordering a halt to the hostilities—brought the Wisconsin Irish together again. The Radical Republicans opposed to President Andrew Johnson used the outrage among the Irish in Wisconsin to their advantage, leading to an unusual sight in 1866 when Irish cheered wildly at a Republican mass meeting called by Milwaukee city councilor Centre Burke.

Irish nationalism was one major factor influencing Irish political opinion in Wisconsin—religion was the other. Being foreign and Catholic made the Irish doubly suspicious in the minds of the Anglo political establishment and made them targets of nativist bigotry. German Catholics were less a target of Yankee hostility in Wisconsin because the long history of Irish-English hostility colored Anglo opinion of the Irish. German Protestants had serious reservations about joining with the Irish to counter the anti-foreign machinations of the Know-Nothing Party—a populist party with strong anti-Catholic, anti-immigrant and racist leanings. The anti-clerical German liberal, Bernard Domschke asserted:

The idea of forming a union of foreigners against Nativism is wholly wrong and destroys the possibility of any influence on our part; it would drive us into union with the Irishmen, those American Croats. In our struggle we are not concerned with nationality, but with principles; we are for liberty and against union with Irishmen who stand nearer barbarism and brutality than civilization and humanity. The Irish are our natural enemies, not because they are Irishmen, but because they are the truest guards of popery.

Despite the hatred directed at their religion, the Irish Catholic remained devout; Catholicism was part of what made them Irish. It also kept them from embracing the Republican Party. Wisconsin Germans, by contrast, were more diverse in their religious beliefs. There was an anticlerical contingent who held radical political beliefs—the Forty-Eighters (the name derived from their participation in the anti-monarchical revolutions that swept Europe in 1848), Lutherans, and other smaller Protestant sects—that often felt more at home in the Republican Party. The Irish were religiously more homogenous and that homogeneity mirrored their strong support for the Democratic Party. Grace McDonald has claimed, "Irish allegiance to the Democratic party became a tradition among them, so much so that an Irish Democrat turned Republican was considered almost as much a social outcast as an Irish Catholic who gave up his Faith."

This strong attachment to the Democrats meant that the Irish in Wisconsin had few opportunities to gain access to political power since the Democratic Party was the minority party in Wisconsin for most of the period after the Civil War. Other factors also worked against an Irish political machine obtaining control of the levers of power in the state. Chief among these was the comparatively few Irish compared to the number of Anglo-Americans, Germans, and Norwegians. The percentage of Irish in Wisconsin decreased as the nineteenth century progressed. In Milwaukee—where the Irish once held sway and which produced shrewd politicians in the traditional Irish mode such as John White and Timothy O'Brien—the Third Ward became a haven for newly arriving Italian immigrants. The Poles, too, displaced the balance of power the Irish held in city politics. However, even as a minority among minority groups, the Irish were important in Wisconsin politics in the nineteenth century. They were able politicians and administrators and many held office on the local level. They were necessary to the success of the Democratic Party, and the Republicans, realizing their political savvy and bloc-voting patterns, often tried to woo them to their side.

The decline of the Irish political contingent in Milwaukee came about through a tragic accident. On September 8, 1860, the lumber schooner *Augusta* plunged into the side of the steamer *Lady Elgin* on Lake Michigan. The *Lady Elgin* sank and sent more than three hundred Irish men and women from Milwaukee to a watery grave. The cream of the Irish Democrats in Milwaukee had set out on an excursion to Chicago on the *Lady Elgin* to hear Stephen Douglas, their candidate for president of the United States, speak at a rally. The boat sank off the bluffs near Winnetka, Illinois, on its return trip. In his book on the disaster, C.M. Scanlan claimed, "As the Irish in Milwaukee seemed to be in the ascendancy at that time, the accident forever pushed them into the background, there, as most of the people lost were young Irishmen and Irishwomen." Grace McDonald echoed this assessment, "September 8, 1860 marked the beginning of a decline in the Irish population of Milwaukee." While demographic shifts were a more important reason for this downturn, the wreck of the *Lady Elgin* was certainly a tragic component of the decline of the Irish in Wisconsin.

In the twentieth century, the Irish continued to vote more for the Democratic Party than the Republican Party (or other parties), but their strong allegiance and the reasons for it were beginning to change. The Irish were losing many of their distinctive political views. Irish nationalism faded as a determiner of political affiliation—particularly after Ireland gained independence, to a certain extent, in 1922. Irish support for World War I was lukewarm because the United States was allied with Great Britain, but the fire of the Fenian days was mostly extinguished. The Irish were assimilating; gone were the days of the Bloody Third and Fourth Wards. The Irish in Wisconsin today are statistically similar to their neighbors in voting patterns. No longer can we speak of an Irish bloc or of the Irish voting the straight Democratic ticket. Voting as Wisconsinites rather than as an Irish voting bloc, the Irish did, however, continue to support agendas that fit in well with traditional Irish concerns. Maude McCreery, the Wisconsin suffragist and social reformer who was honored in a St. Patrick's Day proclamation by President Bill Clinton in 1999, upheld the Irish political tradition of advocating social reform and the cause of the underdog. She was an active worker in the Socialist

Party, the Milwaukee Federated Trades Council, and the Farm-Labor-Progressive Federation, as well as an accomplished journalist and an area organizer for the American Federation of Labor. The controversial Joseph McCarthy, U.S. Senator from Appleton and crusader against communism, was popular in Irish working-class neighborhoods across the country. His brand of anti-communism was also found in the Irish hierarchy of the American Catholic Church. Many would be surprised to learn of the support for Senator McCarthy among the Irish in Ireland during that time. One letter written to an Irish Catholic newspaper defended the Senator against his detractors in America: "Everyone knows the great job Senator Joseph McCarthy is doing in fighting Communist infiltration in government. Only recently, the Bishop of Cork, after a visit to America revealed the courageous fight McCarthy has made against Communism. It is the duty of the Catholic . . . not to sit idle, or remain indifferent to this attack on a fellow Irishman and Catholic of whom we are proud."

※

RELIGION AND CULTURE

Faith of our fathers, living still
In spite of dungeon, fire and sword -
O how our hearts beat high with joy
Whene'er we hear that glorious word!
Faith of our fathers, holy faith,
We will be true to thee till death!
"Faith of Our Fathers," by Frederick Faber

Because of their numbers, there is a tendency to focus on Irish Catholics in Wisconsin. But there were pockets of Protestant Irish around the state; some Irish Protestant communities could be found in Lima Township, Rock County; Koshkonong Township, Jefferson County; and Exeter in Green County. Of the 11 percent who claim Irish heritage in Wisconsin today, no doubt many do not profess the Catholic faith. That probably has less to do with settlements of Irish Protestants in Wisconsin, than to the nature of modern society. Intermarriages, conversions, and migration from other states all have had an effect on the number of Protestants in Wisconsin who claim Irish ancestors.

Irish Protestants left their mark on Wisconsin. James Douglas MacBride was born in Co. Down and came to this country in June of 1803, during a period when Protestant emigration was relatively high. He first settled in Pittsburgh, but around 1842 or 1843 MacBride visited Madison. He was so taken with its location that he purchased a tract of five hundred acres on the eastern shore of Lake Mendota. He was a founding member of the First Presbyterian Church of Madison and he lent his name to the promontory on the eastern part of Lake Mendota. At one time called McBride's Point, it now goes by the name Maple Bluff.

Although the Protestant story is an important one, it is the history of Irish Catholic immigration that has contributed the bulk of the Irish story in Wisconsin. Irish Catholics in Wisconsin differ from other Irish Catholic settlements in the United States. Almost everywhere the Irish went in the United States, they were able to gain control of the Catholic Church hierarchy. In Wisconsin they did not because the church hierarchy was mostly composed of Germans. This led to tensions between Irish and German clergy and it also caused problems for the laity of both nationalities. The Irish clergy often found themselves blocked from bishoprics—including the most important one, pastoring the Archdiocese of Milwaukee. In 1878 when Archbishop John Martin Henni, a German, was aged, infirm, and in need of a coadjutor bishop who would then be in line to succeed him, he chose Bishop Michael Heiss of LaCrosse, also a German. This caused certain members of the Irish clergy to petition Archbishop James Gibbons of Baltimore, a man with some clout in Rome, for an English-speaking coadjutor. They pointed out that all ecclesiastical offices in the state were held by Germans, except one, which was held by a Belgian. While Henni made some concessions to the Irish clergy in other matters, he held firm to his choice of Heiss.

Bishops attempted to be fair to their flock by attempting, when possible, to appoint a parish priest of the same nationality as the majority of congregants. This did not always solve the problem, however, and many communities had two churches—one for the Irish and one for the Germans. A correspondent for the *Boston Pilot*, on observing this parochial arrangement in Wisconsin, remarked:

> It is nothing at all unusual to see an Irish Congregation, comprised of from fifty to two hundred farmers and their families living in a circuit of about a mile around their neat little church to which is at-

tached a few acres of land and the residence of their zealous pastor, and on the next eminence, beyond the stream or grassy marsh, a German church in the midst of a numerous and faithful congregation of industrious farmers, who care very little about becoming Yankeeized, either in language or manners. . . . In no other state have the Irish and German emigrants flocked together, and built up settlements exclusively Irish or German like in it.

As this correspondent implied, the main reason for this division was the language barrier between the two communities, but each religious culture was also different. The Catholic Church is universal but certain beliefs and practices are unique to a culture; to note one example, Irish funeral customs differed from German customs. The result of these differences was that German congregations often split from older Irish parishes. Examples of this development include St. Mary's separating from St. Peter's in Milwaukee in 1847, Holy Redeemer splitting from St. Raphael's in Madison in 1859, and St. Joseph's parting from St. Mary's in Appleton in 1868.

German and Irish Catholics were not constantly bickering, however. Both groups realized the importance of presenting a unified religious front in the face of anti-Catholic prejudice. In disputes between the Catholic hierarchy and the government, the Irish in Wisconsin, for the most part, supported the stance taken by the Catholic hierarchy and followed church leadership of their German bishops. For example, the Bennett Law of 1890 required all schools in the state, including the parochial schools, to teach reading, writing, arithmetic and U.S. History in the English language and demanded that children attend school in the place of their residence. For Irish Catholics, the language requirement was not offensive since they mostly spoke English, but the law threatened the environment of the Catholic schools to set their own lessons and standards and to incorporate either the native language of an immigrant community or the traditional Latin.

The Catholic religion was central to Irish social life as well. The parish church and its surrounding buildings were more than a place to worship; it was a school, a meeting place, the center of social organizations, and the location where the celebratory rites of life were held. In small Irish communities like Monches and Meemes, the parish was the center of almost all activity. Because of its importance, the church was one of the first buildings the Irish built after settling in Wisconsin. No church in a community meant that people had to ride a distance to attend mass in neighboring areas or wait for priests to come to them and celebrate mass in local farmhouses (a common practice in Ireland before the famine). To fulfill the liturgical requirements of the Church, it was necessary to have a church nearby. In Kinnickinnic Township near River Falls, the Catholic community held fairs and other events throughout the 1870s in order to raise the money needed to build a church. They finally were able to build St. Brighid's (later re-named Bridget's), but it took many years after its completion before they had a resident parish priest. Because of their fundraising efforts, the Reardons and Stapletons of Kinnickinnic took an interest in the running and upkeep of the church; it was almost like a second home to them. According to *The Reardon Family History*, the families were so involved in the running of the church that when it later went into severe debt after a major reconstruction project in 1891, the tension between some family members and the parish priest, Fr. Connolly, was so intense that one of the Reardon children was taken to nearby Stillwater to be baptized.

Groups like the Ancient Order of Hibernians and the Catholic Total Abstinence Society were based on the parish level, and they became popular social institutions for Irish Catholics. The latter organization was quite popular in the nineteenth century and its great number of adherents belies the stereotype of the drunken Irishman. Certainly Irish taverns—places like the Fenian Saloon in Hudson, where a fire started in 1866 that burned much of the town—were popular and served social needs similar to their counterparts in Ireland, but there was also a large number of Irish people who swore off alcohol for religious reasons. The Ancient Order of Hibernians often promoted the Irish nationalist cause and provided a social outlet for Irish men. The Daughters of Erin was a similar organization for women.

Irish life centered on the parish church and Catholic religious beliefs, but that did not mean that there were no other sources of Irish culture. Irish music and storytelling were two customs that carried over into the new world. Before the age of mass entertainment, Irish communities would gather at each other's homes to hear stories and listen to the music of their homeland. Traditional Irish music, with its fast pace and racing beat, was often accompanied by jigs and reels. An Irish fiddler was often the central figure in Irish music and Wisconsin had its share of fine Irish fiddlers, including Tom Croal of Hill Point in Sauk County, who was described by Fred L. Holmes, in his book on ethnic Wisconsin, as the "last of the Irish bards living in Wisconsin." Holmes in his tour of ethnic Wisconsin in the mid-twentieth century, also ran across Timothy Crimmins of Madison who volunteered to show him a bit of Irish traditional culture. "Sure, I'll jig for ye, if ye come around tonight when my friend, Red Jack O'Connor is over with his fiddle. When I was young, I would have been the champeen except for a little error. I still have my old hat and fiddle that I brought over from Ireland."

THE DISAPPEARING IRISH
AND IRISH RESURGENCE

The Cadillac stood by the house
And the yanks they were within
And the tinker boys they hissed advice
'Hot-wire her with a pin'
We turned and shook as we had a look
In the room where the dead men lay
So big Jim Dwyer made his last trip
To the home where his father's laid . . .
Fare thee well gone away
There's nothing left to say
'cept to say adieu
To your eyes as blue
As the water in the bay
And to big Jim Dwyer
The man of wire
Who was often heard to say
I'm a free born man of the USA

"The Body of an American, " by Shane McGowan

As the nineteenth century progressed the percentage of Irish people settling in Wisconsin decreased. After the initial surge around the time of the famine, Irish immigration fell off rather drastically. The Germans, who continued to move into the state throughout the nineteenth century, outnumbered the Irish by two to one in 1860. Norwegians and Poles also started to come into the state in larger numbers at this time. The Irish were losing their percentage share of Wisconsin's population.

By the turn of the century, many of the Irish had moved or were beginning to move to other states. The Reardons and Stapletons saw some of their sons and daughters move to fill jobs in the lumber mills of Minnesota or to purchase cheap land in the Dakotas. Later generations moved to Chicago to work in the entertainment field or to attend school. This was a common development in the story of the Irish in Wisconsin. In the early part of the twentieth century local newspapers wrote about the changing Irish communities. In 1926 the *Milwaukee Journal* wrote of an abandoned Irish settlement, "Shacks, decayed and fallen in, are the only traces left of the habitation of St. Martin's island, a beautiful tract lying between the Door county peninsula and Michigan by a colony of Irish fishermen over 50 years ago." In 1931 the *La Crosse Tribune and Leader Press* ran an article on an area known as Irish Coulee that observed, "There isn't an Irishman in the narrow confines of the valley today, where once there was one of the few and, perhaps, the only Irish settlement of nearby western Wisconsin." Fred L. Holmes, in his visit to perhaps the most Irish town in Wisconsin—Erin Prairie in St. Croix County—recorded the following observation from the town's assessor: "Erin Prairie has changed mightily since I was a boy. Then the overwhelming majority of the people were native-born Irish or first generation descent. So many of the younger people have gone to St. Paul and Minneapolis, the Irish ways are dying out." Holmes later added his own assessment of developments that saw the Irish moving off the farms and into the cities. "With the passing of the pioneers, customs have been dropped quite generally and the younger generations are rapidly losing their Irish identity."

How do we square the numbers that show the Irish in the late nineteenth and early-twentieth century losing demographic ground to the Germans, Scandinavians, and Poles, with recent studies placing them as the second-largest ethnic group in the state after the Germans? Toward the turn of the twentieth century, the Irish in Wisconsin began to assimilate into the larger American culture. By the 1950s, the vast majority of American citizens no longer considered Catholicism a "foreign" religion out of touch with American values. It had entered the mainstream of American life, and its emergence blunted one of the distinctive attributes of the Irish American. The traditional Irish-American affiliation with the Democratic Party also lessened, and Irish political views began to resemble the views of their neighbors. When Ireland (minus its northeast corner) won independence from Great Britain, Irish nationalism began to disappear as well (until the violence of the 1960s in Northern Ireland, which revived nationalist feelings among Irish Americans). What looked like a disappearing Irish culture in Wisconsin during this period was actually an instance of people adjusting to a new socioeconomic status and a new sense of identity.

The last few decades, however, have seen a boom in interest in Irish culture in the state of Wisconsin. And the development of Irish organizations such as the following: The Shamrock Club, the oldest and largest Irish-American organization in Wisconsin, founded in 1960, boasting nine chapters statewide; the Emerald Society, a police organization formed in 1990; the Glencastle Irish Dancers, a school for Irish dancing based in Milwaukee and founded in 2000; Milwaukee's branch of the Gaelic League, a club that promotes and preserves the Irish language that has its origins in nineteenth century Ireland; the Milwaukee Hurling Club, begun in 1996 to champion the ancient Irish sport of hurling; the Celtic Music Association of Madison, bringing traditional Celtic music to the city for over twenty years; and the Irish Genealogical Society of Wisconsin, founded in 1992 for the purpose of aiding genealogical inquiry and promoting the study of Irish history and culture. This is not an exhaustive list, but we can see how much of the Irish cultural heritage it covers. Sports, language, music, dance, and genealogy—there are few aspects of Irish culture that cannot be enjoyed in the state of Wisconsin today.

Far from losing their Irish identity as Fred L. Holmes claimed of an earlier generation, today's descendants living in Wisconsin find outlets beyond traditional nationalism and Catholicism to express their Irish roots. Pride among Irish Americans in Wisconsin leads them to take an interest in traditional music and dance or to learn the sport of hurling. This pride also leads them to identify themselves as Irish when surveys are taken. Many of the names on the membership rolls of these organizations are not traditionally Irish, but even one Irish ancestor is enough for some people to identify themselves as such. Irish culture, far from standing out from the rest of U.S. culture, contributes to the American experience. The St. Patrick's Day parades across the state are both a celebration of ethnic pride and an all-American event. Irish culture in Wisconsin today is inclusive instead of exclusive.

Wisconsin is also a center of serious scholarly work undertaken on Ireland and Irish topics. Myles Dillon, son and grandson of two of the most influential Irish nationalist politicians of their times (his grandfather was John Blake Dillon, founder of the influential nationalist newspaper the *Nation* and his father John Dillon was a leading figure in the Irish Home Rule movement), was a professor of Gaelic and Irish history and literature at the University of Wisconsin-Madison in the 1930s and 1940s. During his tenure, he donated a collection of Gaelic manuscripts from the eighteenth and nineteenth centuries to the university—a rather rare collection for an American university to possess. Some of the top scholars in the field of Irish Studies have worked and continue to work in Wisconsin. Indicating the strength of the local Irish studies community, both Marquette University in Milwaukee and the University of Wisconsin–Madison have hosted the annual American Conference of Irish Studies meeting, which gathers the top academics in the field to discuss their work while also showcasing famous Irish poets and musicians and providing a forum for Irish politicians.

There are many Irish places to be found in Wisconsin, from communities whose very names sound like a blend of Ireland and Wisconsin—Erin Prairie comes to mind—to places like Darlington, Shullsburg, and Williams Bay that don't sound at all Celtic but had the highest number of people claiming Irish ancestry in the 2000 census. Perhaps the best place to return to end this brief study is on Milwaukee's lakefront, where the clans gather every August for Irish Fest and a celebration of identity. From its debut in 1981, this festival has grown into an organization that throughout the year supports all aspects of Irish culture, provides scholarships that promote Irish heritage, and houses a huge archive of recorded Irish and Irish-American Music. (Irish Fest has sponsored the publication of this book, in part, and several programs in conjunction with the book's printing.) The festival has grown into the largest Irish festival in the country. Walking among the festival-goers who are learning the Irish language, watching the currach (an Irish fishing boat) races, listening to Irish music, and enjoying the food and drink, one gets the sense of how much interest there is in things Irish among Wisconsinites. One also realizes that this state, so closely associated with the Germans, Scandinavians, and Poles, has more than a wee bit of Gaelic spirit.

Left: Edward Ryan (1819–1880), born in County Meath, was a Democrat completely opposed to Lincoln, whose political career seemed to evaporate after the end of the war. He returned to public life in 1873 when he mounted a vigorous attack on state railroad policies, and the next year was appointed Chief Justice of the State Supreme Court.

State of Wisconsin.

WILLIAM R. TAYLOR, Governor.

To All to Whom these Presents shall Come, Greeting:

Know Ye, That reposing special Trust and Confidence in the Integrity and Ability of Edward G. Ryan of Milwaukee *I have appointed him* Chief Justice of the Supreme Court of The State of Wisconsin Vice Luther S. Dixon resigned.

And I do hereby authorize and empower him to execute and to fulfill the duties of that trust according to his best discretion, until his successor is elected and qualified.

unless the Governor of this State for the time being shall think proper sooner to revoke and determine this Commission.

In Testimony Whereof, *I have hereunto subscribed my name and caused the Great Seal of the State of Wisconsin to be affixed.*

Done at Madison, This Sixteenth *day of* June *, in the year of our Lord one thousand eight hundred and seventy-* Four.

W. R. Taylor

By the Governor: Peter Doyle

Secretary of State.

On June 16, 1874, Edward Ryan became the head of the state's legal community, signed into law by Governor Taylor and Secretary of State Peter Doyle. Ryan remained Chief Justice for six years until his death in 1880.

Patrick Cudahy (1849–1919) from County Kilkenny, arrived in Milwaukee as an infant and grew up calling the Cream City his home. He made his fortune in the meat packing business, founding a new industrial city named Cudahy. He was active in the Ancient Order of Hibernians and the Friends of Irish Freedom.

PH 2

PH 2127 (3), p.71

"Uncle Sam's Lodging House" a cartoon by Keppler, appeared on the pages of *Puck*, June 7, 1882, capturing nearly every stereotype that the Irish (and other ethnic groups) had to endure, from a completely belligerent manner, to simian facial characteristics, to a bottle of rye tucked into the bed.

CF 186

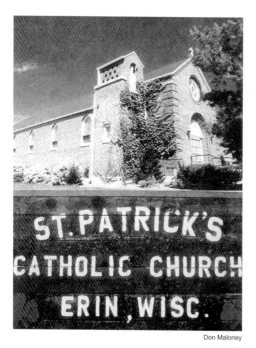

Don Maloney

Top: Tunneling through walls of rock to build the railroad was an arduous, back-breaking job, one which many immigrant groups shared in the state of Wisconsin, although the first tracks were more likely to have been built by the Irish as they arrived in large numbers before many other immigrant groups. These railroad workers appear by their handiwork in May 1898 when more northern track was being laid.

Left: Some communities never lost their strong sense of ethnic identity. St. Patrick's Church in Erin Prairie continues to embrace its Irish sensitivities. The original church was built in 1869.

WHi (W6) 7233

In Queenstown, Ireland, immigrant groups prepare to leave their homeland. This group left Ireland in the late nineteenth century, much later than those who arrived in Wisconsin.

PH 6022

Senatorial candidate Joe McCarthy shaking the hand of Wisconsin Governor Walter Goodland, August 16, 1946. McCarthy's defeat of "Young Bob" La Follette ended that family's tenure in the U.S. Senate. McCarthy ran, in part, on his appeal to blue collar voters.

PH 3729

Wisconsin native Georgia O'Keefe received a Governor's Arts Award from Warren Knowles, ca. 1967.

David Power

David Power

Above left: Members of the Gogin clan pose for a portrait: Standing are four of the ten siblings, from left, Ella Gogin, Jim Gogin, Mary Conway, and Mabel Kileen; seated are their parents, County Cork natives Richard (on left) and Anna Cooke Gogin (on right); sitting in between them is one of their many grandchildren, Dot Carey.

Right: Mabel Gogin Kileen was the youngest of the ten children, and like her elder sisters taught and worked outside the home, a characteristic more common to Irish immigrant women than any other group.

David Power

Art Gogin, the youngest brother in the Gogin family, owned this home in Red-granite, 1908.

David Power

Pine River in Waushara County, home to the Gogin family farm.

David Power

Brother and sister John and Gertie Gogin pose together, ca. 1885.

THE LETTERS OF THE GOGIN FAMILY, 1877–1908

The Gogin family history, a part of which is captured in these fifteen letters written between 1877 and 1908, reflects the typical Irish experience in Wisconsin during the latter half of the nineteenth century. The letters are from Manuscript Collection M99-049, housed at the Wisconsin Historical Society, and the collection includes sixteen letters (the sixteenth letter is fragmentary and not does not appear here) as well as a scrapbook, essays, newspaper clippings, a photograph, and a small notebook, among other small items. The correspondents are all siblings, six of the nine surviving children of Richard Gogin (b. 1830) and Anna Cooke Gogin (b. 1832). Richard and Anna were both natives of County Cork and immigrated separately to the northeastern United States. They met in Philadelphia and married there in 1855. After the wedding, they traveled to Wisconsin by oxcart, arriving in Waushara County where all of their ten children would be born, beginning with Mary (Mollie) in 1856, and ending with Mabel in 1878.

Anna and Richard's married life is not the focus of the letters but later family history revealed that Richard spent nearly eighteen months away from the family farm in Pine River from February of 1864 to July of 1865 when he served as a private in Company B of the 16th Wisconsin Volunteers. With his regiment, he accompanied Sherman on his March to the Sea. Ten months after his return, Anna gave birth to their fifth child, John William Sherman Gogin, a living monument to Richard's Civil War experience.

It was eleven year-old John who wrote the first letter in the series, a letter to his oldest sister, twenty-one year-old Mollie, who was also his teacher. It is to Mollie that the majority of the letters in this group were written, and although they covered an array of topics and numerous digressions and details, some regular themes emerged. Work and job opportunities were a constant topic throughout the letters, beginning with the work of the five Gogin daughters, all of whom appear to have taught school at some point in their lives. Many young women from various ethnic backgrounds taught in the western frontier's one-room schoolhouses, but working independently of the family is a practice that Irish women embraced far more often than their immigrant sisters, both as teachers and domestic servants.

Of the sons, young Richard also worked a traditionally "Irish" job, on the railroad, but unlike the men of his father's generation, Richard had the opportunity to work on something other than building the railroad. He served as telegraph operator for the St. Paul, Minneapolis, and Manitoba Railway. These letter writers also regularly described the work of the family farm, and the needs of the small communities in Waushara County; these needs mirrored those of other agricultural communities all over the state, several of which are listed on the letters themselves as the siblings traveled. The Gogins never directly addressed the state of being Irish, or Irish-American, but their various comments about religion and culture indicate the impact of their faith and family ties in their daily lives. The original spellings and phrasings appear here, revised only for clarification, and italics appear for the underlining they frequently used to emphasize their meaning with one another. Numerous details appear here as well, to allow readers to appreciate the everyday life of an Irish family in Wisconsin a generation after settlement, when assimilation had begun.

Centreville, July 26, 1877

To Mary Gogin teacher,

For my part I am well satisfied, onelly that you have been a little to easy with us sometimes. I think that I have improved grately in most of studies espicely in Arithmetic and Geography; and I think that I have learned still more in the new books; that is in History and Language-lessons. This is not a very long letter but it is about all I can think of.

Yours respectively,

John Gogin

Merry Christmas Happy New Year,
Pine River, Dec 18, 1881

Dear Sister Mollie,

Today is Sunday and I will try and answer your nice long letter. I am just about sick to-day. I do not know *what* ails me, but I feel so dizzy and strange. Sometimes the top of my head feels so light and things swim before my eyes. I have these spells quite often, although I never told anyone before. But when I get over that feeling I never feel better in my life. I have a splendid school this Winter and it hardly seems possible that it's so near out. I thrashed two of the boys one morning, one for disobeying me the other for using vulgar language. You are much mistaken when you think [their youngest sister] Mabel is a good girl in school. She is forever turning around in her seat and giggly. I had to take a *stick* to her one day and I have had to use one on [their brother] Art twice besides making him remain in, stand on the floor, &c. If I turn my back on him *one* minute he is throwing paper wads or into something. I will tell father of him if he keeps on: but it seems natural for him to be tormenting *someone*. Will Lang who lives on the old Lang place, comes to school, he is 19, and *I never* saw anyone *so* bashful, he is not as bad *now* as at first, as I talk with him and do my best to make him feel at home. Lee's sister Dottie is keeping house for him while her husband is in the woods. She is a nice woman. Tell the girls I wish that they and you would come down between Christmas and New Years as I am not going to have a vacation, but I am going to have an *exhibition* on the 29 of Dec. I have it then because [their sister] Gertie is home now and is going to take part. All the neighbors are taking part . . . We meet once a week, in the evening at the schoolhouse, to practice, and we have some *good* pieces. We *expect* to have a nice time, Ambrose Suckey is going to get a crimson curtain for us from the church in Poy Sippi[.] We are going to decorate the school house with evergreen and the girls are each going to get a Chinese lantern to light the stage. Is [Mollie's husband] Henry coming home during the holidays?

Ma . . . [has] gone to church today. I tell you, Maggie Borst looked like a [dandee] in her new costume—it fit to perfection. She got some fancy braid and I used it for a panel down the side as the waist was trimmed in velvet. I made the *bottom* of the skirt *perfectly plain*, blind stitched it, you know, and let it fall over the underskirt and it looked *very* firm, as she got reeds to put in the back. I told her what they were for and she got a set with rubber and buckles attached for 15¢. I finished it the second day that I went there. She had to put the finishing touches on it, that is sew it everywhere I trimmed it. I charged her 75¢ a day and my board and she was willing to pay me more. Ada Mills was so pleased with the fit of it that she wants to get me to cut and fit one for *her*. So she told Anna. I think that picture you sent me was nice, only it is so dark . . . This is every bit of writing paper I have got, so will have to close. Will write more next time. Write soon.

Ella.

[Their brother] Dick sent Art his gun for a Xmas present.

This first long letter from Ella provides a good summary of different family members' status and reveals Ella's fiery personality and drive as well as her entrepreneurial spirit. She is about age 15.

Pine River, July, about 1882

Dear Sister Mollie,

I thought I would celebrate the 4th by writing to *you*, it was rainy this morning so we concluded to remain at home. We may go to Auroraville this afternoon if it clears off. They are having a . . . celebration there. We had thought of going to the lake and having a picnic, but it will be too wet for *that*. Where are you and Henry going to celebrate? Mother and Father were up to the soldier's home on the 21, they had dinner at Johnny Galagher's, he was the first one they met, and insisted on them going to his place so he got into the buggy with them and showed them the way. Ma said she had a nice visit with his wife . . . [and] was delighted with the trip. We received a letter from Dick the other day and he wanted to know when we heard from you as he had not in a long time. He is still at Elk River and feeling well. I had a letter from [their brother] John a short time since and *he* is well. I guess he has made an application to a company in Minneapolis for an elevator for there was a letter came to Pine River last Sat. for a Mr. K. inquiring about John, what kind of a young man he was and whether he was friendly and sociable among farmers. Charlie read it to Pa and answered it and had Pa mail the letter, Pa offered to pay him but he would neither accept it, nor a treat, he said he was always willing to help those who deserved it. Gertie and I went over to Sherlocks Sunday. John is home now, he has about 20 different views (large) of Kimbalton and nearly as many cabinet photographs of the inhabitants including Mr. and Mrs. Kimball, and one of little Kimmy Clark in a brass frame, he said it seemed awful lonesome down here now. He wanted me to go up there and teach this winter. $40 a month and only 13 scholars, he said they had quite a time to procure a teacher last winter. Till O'Brion . . . [wants] me to come . . . and teach sometime, she said their teachers were all hired for the coming year, but they were nearly all teachers from away off, and they never taught but a term or two when they would get married. . . . She said their primary teacher got more than any $600 a year and that *she* did not pass examination but as she was a splendid hand among children they accepted her. You bet I would go this Fall if I had a chance to get a school, But the schools there

begin in September just about the time of examination here, and I want
to get a 2nd grade *here* before I leave this county. I am going to write in
W[a]upaca County this fall if possible. Gertie and I and Ettie attended
school meeting Monday night. We heard that all the ladies were going to
attend but they backed out and Mrs. Clark was the only one who came.
. . . They voted on whether the books would be furnished by the *district*
or the scholars and the latter carried the vote, then they decided to dispose of the books on hand and offered to sell them at once to those who
would bid on them. No one seemed ready to buy so they put them all in
a pile on the table[,] and put the whole business up at auction to be sold
to the highest bidder, and I got them for the sum of $2.21. I knew just
what was there and their value while they were so excited they did not
care, but you bet there has been weeping and gnashing of teeth ever
since. The scholars are to buy them from me or get new ones. I assorted
them over, took a list of them marked the prices, and told them if they
wanted to purchase they could have them at the price marked and if they
thought that *too* much they could leave them, as I was not particular
whether they bought them or not. I was satisfied that I could dispose of
them elsewhere, for *more* than I had offered them for. There are 130 *good*
books and a great many loose ones that I shall burn. Charley and Hat
came over to school the next morning to get some for Harry, and when
Charley saw what a great stack of books I had he was mad as fury. He
said they must have been crazy to just the same as *give* them to me and
then buy them back again. Now he says if you offer them any way *rea-
sonable* we will buy of you of course we are willing for you to *make* a little
on them but we don't propose to let you make a fortune. I says yes sir I
will put them down for what they are worth and I don't care whether you
buy them or not it is all the same to me. I offered him a second reader for
.10 cts and he turned his head away and said he never'd pay that for it,
so I just went about my business, taking down the names and he and Hat
and Ettie talked by themselves a long time. Mart was mad a blazes too. I
told her they would have done the same if they had a chance, that it was
none of my business what they done with the books, they put them up at
auction and *all* bid on them and *I* got them, with the priviledge of sell-
ing them to the scholars and I didn't see why they were not just as good
now as they were all summer. Well-if they had to buy books they would-
n't buy *"old things."* The trouble was they saw I was going to make something. I told them it was not the *value* of the books I looked at, but it was

worth a good deal to find out what folks were made of. They were all very nice when things went in *their* favor but when any one else got a good thing then they showed their *true* character. I never gave them an inch, but stood my ground and let them see they could neither *bully* or frighten me when I knew I was right. Pa said he was just *glad* I got the books, and glad I was smart enough for *them*. I did not get mad but kept cool and that made them all the madder. I told them I had no ill feeling for any of them. I merely took them for what they were worth, since I had the chance of testing them. Well I have scratched this off full and then "the half has not been told" but good By for this time. (Write soon)

By the way Ettie and I went to the graduation, from there to the old settlers meeting, Poy Sippi and from there to Brushville to a dance in the evening. The dance was a platform at Mr. Godson's and was splendid, such a nice crowd and they are nice folks. I had a sple[n]did time all around, Andrew Jensen took us, he has a top buggy now. The Pine River girls were hopping mad they were *sure* that he was going to take them to the dance, and Milly Wright was goose enough to give *herself* away. Tom took Gertie and I to a dance at the Mill, saw Mrs. Decker, and Wilcox had a nice time in the rain and mud. Give my love to brother Henry.

Ella

Young Richard first appears in this letter, and his request of his older sister for a small loan so that he might enjoy himself is of note because a male family member sought financial assistance of a female member, indicating she had more financial power than he did.

Ripon [November] 30, 1882

Dear Sister Mollie,

You thought that I would not answer your letter for a month or so, so I am going to show you that I can hurry a little even I don't want any money.

I saw Mr. Putnam your boss here about 3 weeks ago and had a letter all ready to send you by him but he was not on the train that he said he was going to be so I did not get a chance to send it. I was all about that "piece of paper business" it but will have to tell it over again. . . .

I am glad to hear that Nellie is going to school this winter and hope she will like it and get along well. How do you like your school now[?] I hope you don't have any trouble with them.

You wanted me to send you Nell's directions but I will have to get them myself first and I don't know whether I will or not. I guess she has got mad at me for some reason or other. I went down to the train to bid her good bye and she said she would send her address but I have not got it yet. She told me all about that quarrel they had with the M'y girls. If it is so I think they acted kind of mean. I wish I had been there to see the fun myself.

I spoke about not wanting any money when I began my letter but I shall have to have some before long as my month is up pretty soon. That is the 2nd but I expect a letter from home soon. I wish you could lend me a little to have for spending money as I think it would do me good to have a little fun once in a while and it is fearful hard work to keep from going to dances or anything at all. It would kind of keep me from having the blues. They . . . are going to start a regular school of Telegraphy here, so I will have to leave the office and go there and I don't know whether I shall like it or not. The man that is going in with this operator is that little humpbacked Brushey who used to live in Pine River he is a real nice man and I think will do better by us than the one we are learning of now. I am beginning to like it better every day and I can receive faster now than any one who started in with me.

Today is Thanksgiving and I had turkey for dinner. There is a big dance here in town to night but I am not going. I have only been to one dance since I have been here and I would like to have some money to go to one Christmas anyway. So if you can send me some I will pay you back when my ship comes in as when I get to be president of some Rail road. I went to get me a coat and vest with that money Steve left for me so I can't have any of that for spending money.

. . . I would like to come home Christmas but guess I can't. I would like to go and have a good hunt. Is there any wolves there this winter. Has father got the wind mill up yet.

If I were you you bet I would thump away at that Organ all the time till I learned to play something. I wish I could get a chance.

Well this is a pretty long letter for me and as it is getting late will have to bring it to a close by sending best wishes to all the folks at home. I have got to be such a fearful old scribbler and wrot[e] this so fast that I can hardly read it myself and the next time you write you want to write with a pen. I could hardly read your last letter. If you get acquainted with Net

Beaman tell her hello! for me. Kiss [their youngest sister] Mabel also for
me when you see her, from

Brother Dick.

In this letter, Ella featured illness and death of both neighbors and the animals on
the farm as an ongoing topic. The reference to a telephone call should not be too
surprising as the telephone had been invented more than twenty years earlier. The
brief mention of relatives from Philadelphia was the only reference in the group of
letters to family still in the east.

Centerville, Wis, Sunday Jan 21, 1883

Dear Sister [Mollie],

As we have been waiting to hear from you and not receiving any letter I thought I would scratch a few lines to you. We are all well and hope
you are the same. We have not heard from Dick yet. Gertie wrote to him
Thursday as she staid home. Has he wrote to you yet. A week ago today
Elsie Cotanch was buried. Father, mother, Artie and I went to the funeral.
[Their brother] Jim went out to get the team ready to go to the funeral,
he found Charley loose he had kicked the colts. Flora was not cut bad
but a little piece of hide was taken off. But he put a terrible cut in the
fleshy part of Dollies leg. Sherlock said it should be sewed up but we could
not get a flesh needle any nearer than Berlin so they put on tar to keep
out the cold. They use a wash now of saltpreter, proof of spirits, and
water put on with a syringe. I was down to see it the other day and my it
is terrible. The flesh is hanging in chunks and it was all blood. It will not
make her lame but it will leave a bad scar. . . . I have got two letters from
Mary Shingsby in about a week. They read in the paper about an R.
Gogin being burned in the Milwaukee fire so she wrote the second letter
to see if it was Dick. Ben Bass saw the name and thought the same thing,
he telephoned to Ripon to see if he was there and Dick answered him
back. Ben was telling father about it. Mary said Will Heany is clerking in
a store in [Argoville or Argusville]. He told her he read in the paper about
Eddie Kimball being shot. We got a letter from Aunt Maggie . They are
all well[,] little Annie sent mother a ham, some New Years card. She sent
auntie Ellen directions. She said aunt Julia and her husband came out two
years ago, that they went from there to Philadelphia, that if they wrote
to us to give them no encouragement to come out here as they got enough

of them, said she would write more about them next time. She said auntie Ellen was so fat she didn't get over very often to see her. Well I am afraid her ears will burn if I say any more about her so I must change the subject. When auntie Kate wrote last she said to let mother wear that brown skirt of hers. When we took the letter to school to Nellie she wanted to know if we seen what her mother said about the skirt, she acted as if she wanted to keep it and said that it was silk poplin and that you said would make it over for auntie. She has been staying with [their sister] Annie for over two weeks. She was alone for a week or so but Henry is home now so she might come home but she will stay as long as Anna lets her wear her stockings and under clothes. Mother says she is staying away to see if we will forget about the skirt but mother says she needent fret as she don't want it and wont take it. Clinton's head is all broke out like [unreadable]'s was. Mamie's leg is better. Well it's getting dark and as this is my second letter today I must stop. With love from all.

Write soon

Ella.

Be sure and let me know what night you are coming. One Friday night after supper Ned began to bark like fury and I happened to think of what you told me and I tell you I was frightened as every thing was in a mess. I have not told anyone about it.

Good night

Ella.

In these two letters, Dick responded to news from home, perhaps the "other letter" Ella referred to in the previous letter, and continued his descriptions of the social demands of a single young man of twenty-two, living on his own in Ripon, where dances, photograph exchanges, and letters to young ladies occupied his thoughts.

Ripon, Jan 21, 1883

Dear sister Mollie,

I had begun to think you were never going to write to me and I haven't heard from home either since I left[.]

I was terribly surprised to hear of Mrs. Ferrills death. Ed's sister is Mr Kusheys[?] step mother. He was very much surprised too when I told him. It must make [unreadable] feel terrible. I have written twice to Maggie Johnson and have not received an answer yet. . . . I don't know which place she gets her mail, but if she is going to stay with Viola she won't be able to come and learn. but I think she might [answer] my letter any way. I think you might have told me what you heard about that Riponite. I suppose Mag gave me a big breeze [the cold shoulder] and if you could hear Sarah . . . I expect she would give me a bigger one. but I don't care. I am not having a bit of fun this winter. Have you heard about that dance on the 25th in Rn. I just got an invite yesterday and would like to go [awful] well. and I rather think I shall. Although I had promised to go to one here the same night. Are you going to be there. I hope you will If I go can't you mange to come. Were yo[u] to the dance in P.R. [Pine River] Irene and Mag Morrisey were there. I wonder who they went with. Did you hear? was Bill or Jim there. Has father drawn the hay yet from there. I am glad to hear that you liked your school so well. and if you can get it next summer I would take it on preference to the Mt. Morris school. I think that is a pretty rough set over there. Was our folks at the funeral where was she buried.

I suppose she had a very large funeral. Have you had any pictures taken[.] Earnest says he will willingly trade with you[.] He has got some taken lately and says he wont send me one 'til I get some taken too.

My this is a fearful cold day[.] I sit with my back within a few inches of the stove and there I'm freezing it was 50° below here. Is Mary Tice well yet. have you got acquainted with Net Beaman yet. I think she is just about right. Had a big time with her at Will Culver's one night at a dance. My I want to go to that dance [awful] bad but it will cost like everything. I haven't heard from Nell since she left. guess she has got mad at me about some thing, for she promised to write and send her Photo. Can take 25 or 26 words a min. now, but it comes very slowly. Well I hope I will see you at the dance

So bye bye. Dick.

Ripon, Feb 4, 1883

Dear Sis., [Ella]

I was glad to get such a long letter from you but it was news to me to hear that B. B. telephoned to me. I hadn't heard anything of it and asked the operator here and he said that he hadn't heard anything of it either. I didn't see anything of it for 2 or 3 days after the fire or else I should have been scared myself for fear it might have been father. Well I hope Mother got her teeth but like you can hardly believe it. As to Nell Mc. *I* haven't heard from her and don't know where she is, but she promised to write first and send her photo so you bet I won't write till she does.

I got a letter from Ernest last week and he sent me his photo . . . He looks awful sober. He said he had one ready for you as soon as he got yours. Have you had it taken yet? I haven't. If I could afford it I would have some taken this week, for I expect I will not be here very much longer and would like to have some taken before I go, for if I had some I could change. Jeff expects to start for Moorehead Minn tomorrow or next day to take an office there. He is going to try and get me a place there too. I hope he can. It is right across the river from Fargo. . . . Won't it be jolly if I can go out there. If I go it won't cost a cent. They will give me a pass.

I wish you had told me that secret. Of *course* I won't tell. You aren't going to get married are you Eh! I can't think what else it might be. Talk about my being *smitten*. I wouldn't give 2 cents a bunch for all the girls from here to Bedlam only to have fun with and I had just as soon flirt with a girl that is engaged (or married either for that matter) as one that never thought of such a thing. . . . I don't hardly know what John's affect was on going to Ripon he didn't stay only a few hours. Has he really bought the Half[?] place. If so he and Mag. will surely be married before long. I hate to ask it but if you can spare it I wish you—well I won't either. You'd say that's all he wrote for. If you get your photos and send 2 to me I will get one of Ea's for you. Have you made up your mind which school to take yet.

I got a letter from home about the same time you did. They are having fearful times he with the railroads on account of the snow. The operators have to stay up all night. That'll be fun. Well be sure and write soon.

Dicky
Ducky
Dee

Almost six years later to the day of his last letter, Dick again wrote his sister Mollie but the tone had changed from a light-hearted lad of twenty-one to a despairing man of twenty-eight. After many successful years working for the railroad, Dick had bought out the share of a business of a trusted man named Ed Brennan, and he had briefly co-owned a store with another man, "a good Catholic partner" named Donohue. In first working with the accounts after buying into the business,

Dick learned that his new interests were in serious and immediate financial trouble, and soon after learned that Donohue was a serious alcoholic, whose destructive behavior was the source of the store's failure. Dick sent Ed Brennan's letter to Mollie to ask for her opinion on whether Brennan was trustworthy or not.

St. Paul Station, 2-8-1889

My Dear Sister Mollie,

I've started a half a dozen letters to you & my courage has failed me each time for *I* am suffering mental torture enough & I hate to cause you to suffer too, but would have to tell you sometime & may as well do so now. We have failed already & I'm afraid I'm going to lose nearly everything I have saved for so long, & it is breaking my heart for I had counted *so* much on making myself a home with it & to see my hopes dashed to Earth in so short a time has nearly killed me.

The last five weeks have been harder on me than as many years should have been and the humiliation is worse to me than the loss of the money. Mollie the good Catholic partner I was so confident of being associated with has turned out to be one of the meanest, most contemptible, low . . . scoundrels that it has ever been my misfortune to meet & before I knew it he had squandered & stolen so much that we [are] entirely crippled & to save anything at all had to close & the sheriff is now in possession of the store & God only knows whether I'll get a dollar out of it or not. A great many tell me that Ed Brennan won't see me lose everything but as he is bound to be a heavy loser too I'm afraid that I'll not save a thing. He is away in Texas sick a bed & can do nothing for me until he comes home & that may never be as he is very sick. Mollie this has been the worst part of my grief-how I was to tell you and the folks at home, for heavens sake don't tell them yet a while & in time I'll be able to tell them something as when we get this man Donohue out we may possibly start up again although the chances are against it. I commenced New Years to keep the books and the first thing I discovered irregularities but didn't think much about them as thought they could be explained but everywhere I looked I'd find one thing worse than another & found besides that he had overdrawn his account $500. In the five months he had been in business & was running saloon & cigar & drug store bills for over $200, besides lending to his fast friends over $100, in clean cash.

Mollie when I found out the real state of affairs I was almost crazy & tried to take immediate steps to stop it but he got hold of over a hundred and went on a drunk for 3 days, & spent it all then we had to shut the store. It makes my blood boil so when I think of how hard I worked & broke myself down to earn this money & how much we all need & how hard father & all the rest of us are working & then to think that this worse than thief has spent it in carousing & high living it is all I can possibly do to keep from shooting him dead. I had so much faith in Ed Brennan's word that I would have staked my life as quickly as my money on what he said & the same with Johnnie O'Connor & to have it come out this way is another cross for me to bear. Ed declares in a letter to me that he didn't know of a single thing against Donohue & always supposed him to be an honest man & said that when he came back he would do what was right by me. . . . [T]hey say is worth $150.00 & Ed is an only son so think he ought to do something for me anyway.

One thing I have made some staunch & influential friends on the head of it & I trust in God that all will yet turn out right & in time it may be a good thing for me that all this has happened but at present I am nearly broken down in health and completely broken in spirit & cannot look any of my old acquaintances in the face for I must explain everything if I do . . . it is impossible for me to do so [without] almost breaking down. I was so proud of my apparent success in life & knew that it would please mother & father so much & now to have it go this way is a terrible bitter pill for me to swallow. Mollie pls don't let this miserable thing worry you & perhaps I'm a bum for telling you but I had to go to someone for sympathy & knew I must tell you sooner or later. Thank God I saved your $200 and Auntie Kate's $500. If I had lost that too I don't know as I should have been alive today. Yourself & John are the only ones I have told & pls be sure not to even hint anything of this so Mother will hear it for I don't know what effect it might have on her.

I can't write any more this time but if there is anything at all bright turns up will write you at once.

Pls don't worry Mollie as it may come out better than I think
Bro Dick.
Please send Ed's letter back *quickly*

Feb 14-89

Dear Sister Mollie,
Your welcome letter read last evening and am very glad that you look at the matter so philosophically and I praise God that it will not be so bad

as I have thought it would but the prospects at present are that it will be even worse but am keeping up my courage as best I can under the circumstances and hope for the sake of mother & father more than for myself that things may brighten up a little before long. I know Mollie it is almost a mortal sin for me to give way so & whine like a schoolboy over what has befell so many much smarter men before me and in fact just the very thing that has been the making of thousands but no one can realize until they have gone through it what it is to see ones whole prospects [in] life vanish in a few short weeks through no fault of their own only as you say trusting too much to other peoples honesty. I sent you Ed's letter so that you can see for yourself about what kind of man he is and I yet have all the confidence in the world in his honesty of purpose in this matter. Pls be sure to send the letter back to me as I may need it if I have to force matters any. As for Johnny O'Connor there is not a more honest or conscientious man in Dakota and he feels terribly bad over the way things have turned out. I do not blame him one particle for he thought he was doing me a kindness and but for this man Donohue being such a wolf in sheep's clothing everything would have been just as I have been wishing to be for a long time & we could have been independent in a few years. I lay down to sleep thinking possibly when I woke up things may look brighter but when I wake all comes to me in to miserable reality and nearly makes me crazy when I think how things *are* & what they might have been. Know I'm comparatively young & stronger than perhaps a great many but I never can go through again what I have gone through to save the money I have lost and by the time I do, I'll be a miserable crusty old good for nothing. I've always prided myself on being a little ahead of the average operator who is knocking around the world & don't care whether he gets ahead or not and now to think that after these years of saving I'm not a bit better than or farther ahead than the most dissipated of them nearly breaks me down. Don't think you had better tell Gertie anything about it for a while anyway. I wrote John and send him your letter. We'll know something more definite in a week or so & will write you again then. I am a thousand times obliged for your offer of the money but don't think will need it as it will be impossible for me to start up again in business. . . . Trusting in God hoping for the best & to hear from you soon.

Will close
Bro Dick

*Other family members remained oblivious to Dick's financial problems as this let-
ter from nineteen-year-old Gertie indicated. She too had launched a teaching career
that was going to take her to the Dakota Territory, although not permanently, for
she expressed an interest in classes at the State Normal School in Oshkosh, one of
several teacher training institutions, and she wanted to study under a certain in-
structor, although she hinted that there was more than intellectual interest between
them.*

Pine River, Apr. 10, 1889

Darling Sister Mollie,

I received your letter Monday but haven't had *time* to ans. it since[.]
I'm going west sure enough and I do want you to come down . . . if you
can possibly. My school will begin May 1st so . . . I'll only have [two]
weeks after this and this week I'm going to Normal.

I must get a certificate here and they will endorse it in . . . June when
they will have an ex. [an official] there. I'm boarding at Dr. Jewell's. . . .
I'm writing this at noon and will soon have to go back to school so will
not write much. I began Monday. Charles Robinson did also and I tell
you Mollie . . . that he is *so smart* I could listen to him talk all day and
when he gets to be *superintendent* I'm coming back from Dak[ota] to go to
Normal and write under him. I'm not acquainted yet but I hardly ever
look at him (and I do it rather often) but I catch his eye and we both look
the other way and smile. . . .

Well I tell you all the news when [we meet again] which I hope won't
be long . . .

You[r] loving Sister.
Gertie

*Ella also remained oblivious to Dick's financial distress, even stating that a recent
letter from him indicated he was well. Ella congratulated Mollie on her move to
Michigan, and discussed her own upcoming move to Dakota Territory, which was
likely for teaching. Ella, Gertie, and John ultimately would each stake a tree claim.
Ella seemed to have a gift for ending a long, newsy note with a startling piece of
information.*

Pine River, June 30, 1889

Dear Sister Mollie,

Your letter of the 21 is at hand and you don't know how glad we all
were to hear that you had settled down at last and hope nothing may

happen to mar the happiness of your little home. Pa thinks that Henry could do no better than go into the milk business at *that* price or even 3¢.

It seems that you are a long ways from home to think you are in Michigan. Now I would like to walk in and see that nice little home of yours and better still "That nice little man," now don't be jealous. Mother and [their brother] Jim have gone to church today. Two weeks ago Jim and I went down and I staid until last Sunday. I wanted to visit school. I visited the . . . school two times, heard the oral examinations in botany, and oral examinations of the graduates in English Literature and Commercial Law. Monday was class day and Mary O'Donnell went with me. Mary Fitsmorris had the class history which was quite nice but the class prophesy by Kert Stedman was the *most outlandish* thing I *ever heard[.]* [H]e pictured most of the girls as old hags and dishwashers in Sing Sing, had Hughes and Williams leaders of a "Beer Brigade" and had Williams and Hicks in Hell twice and finally left them there. About Lottie Kimball, who goes with Fred Hathaway, he said "although she made a mask on Leigh Hunt at the party, up at Gertie Gogin's near Pine River, she yet 'hath a way' of her own to keep her Hathaway . . ." She was so mad she could have killed him. There was so much in it about Hell and the devil, that, everyone talked about it for the rest of the week, and all thought it was too degrading for such an occasion, or to be allowed to be repeated in a schoolroom that no *gentleman* would have done it. The teachers had not heard it as he claimed to have written it night before, after going home from the . . . sermon, sitting up until 2 o'clock AM to finished it. I think the devil must have helped him write it, it was black enough. (The bees just hummed for the first time, the largest swarm I ever seen, and Art [placed] them all in a hive now).

Now for the graduation. Mollie's dress was cream cashemere combined with a striped silk of cream and old rose. It was . . . fussy. . . . The rest were all so plain. . . . Kate Guinan's was of cream . . . a pointed basque buttoned . . . the back drapery was just . . . made for Mabel and front was trimmed with watered silk ribbon. Kate's subject was Protection, basic temperance, and *the best* delivered. My, but the[y] cheered her through[.] She was encored but had not the courage to come out far enough for the whole audience to see her again. . . . May Luther's was 2nd best subject. The American girl, past and present, she got in a good point about the "women of the Revolution giving up their favorite beverage for the cause, and that was more than the *men* of *the* enlightened period were willing to do." Wasn't that cute though she said that near the beginning and the men on the stage and a number in the audience clapped their hands. John Hughes had the salutatory, which was short and to the point and *well* delivered although he broke down . . . The valedictory . . . entitled Humpty Dumpty was not a bit good, to my notion[.] Mollie got a bushel basket of flowers altogether, and the rest Ditto.

I visited Carrie Barr's room . . . In the Kindergarten they have no books or recitations at all. I think it is just fine. . . . When I get a start again I'm going to Oshkosh and train for a Kindergarten teacher. Mayme Pierce has gone East to be gone for 4 weeks. Then she and May . . . are going to Indiana to attend a Kindergarten there for 4 weeks. They are both splendid teachers now, but I suppose can learn something in the business yet.

I wrote to Dodson for a school in case there will be a vacancy, which I think there will. I have not got his answer yet, as of course they can not tell yet awhile. I have not told anyone but you as I may not succeed, but I am tired of plugging around in those little country schools. Jim wants me to apply for the Castor school but-good Lord deliver us, *I shant.* We got a letter from cousin Johnnie . . . see if he could find employment north, wants to come. Warner Brown called on us yesterday, just arrived for a short visit. *He* too has got to quite business like, you know he is an operator. We have had letters from Dick, John and Gertie, all are well. Father traded Barney for Perkins' sorrel horse as B. would not work on the mower. . . . Pa also traded Tige to Morrison for a big bony four year old colt, sound but *homely.* He was told by some horse jockeys that Tige would *always* be lame. They had two horses the same way he gave $20 boot money and got $18 on B. The sorrel is a *sound honest horse,* and if Pam had not been going away he would not have traded, but Barney is a nice horse to look at, and may make a difference of $5[0] in his team.

. . . Veness Frisbie killed himself by hanging. Everybody is well and I am *tired* writing. Have *two* more, and this is the 3d.

Love from all to you both.

Lovingly,

Sister Ella

In a surprising turn of events, Dick continued to write to Mollie but in part to chastise her because she had refused to return to him a letter from Brennan, the man who had sold him the failing business. Dick had sent Brennan's letter to Mollie to get her opinion of it, and she had kept it since February. Dick mentioned their

*brothers Jim and John and their own frustrations with and plans for financial suc-
cess, and in the same paragraph compared Ella's and Gertie's ambitions. In the
Gogin family everyone's work seemed to be held in equal importance, no matter the
gender.*

St. Paul Station, July 5, 1889

Dear Sister Mollie,

Read your welcomed letter yesterday. I am more than glad that you
are at last settled down and away from the old lady as you didn't seem to
like her very well. I hope Henry will be able to get into something there
so that he can be at home more and will not be obliged to go on the drive
for it is hard and dangerous work.

I haven't written you before because I've been mad and I'm not entirely over it yet either. I asked you twice if you wouldn't send me that letter Brennan wrote me and don't think you had any excuse for not doing
so and it might have helped me. It would have been a little satisfaction
any way and from it I might have known a little better what to do when
he came back. It looks as if he said something that you don't want me to
see and as if you thought I was as much to blame as any one else in the
matter.

I may be wrong and hope I am but I told you everything and sent
you his letters and think you might have been as open with me and if he
has told you anything that was not so think you might at last have given
me a chance to contradict it. There was nothing whatever left and he
claims he is out a good deal more than I am and can do nothing. I have
learned at least one thing and that is that I don't want any more *friends* &
I'll go it alone from this on and try to take care of myself as well as I can.
As for ambition to try and be somebody I've bid good bye to that too. I
used to love friends who claimed they would do anything for me but now
when it comes to a pinch and I'd like to have them help me out or to get
something better they haven't time.

You see by Jim's letter too how things are going at home and what a
happy family we are all around. To help things along too John has got a
bad dose of the big head and lord only knows when he'll stop. He has
bought a farm or whats worse I expect had to take it to save a loan he had
made from what he says and he may be able to pay for it and may not as
crops are very uncertain in that section. I'm sure he would get along allright he would only go a little slower and not try to do too much in a year

or so. Yes I am proud of Gertie and am sure she will do well. I don't know whether we have used poor Ella exactly right or not for we are all helping Gertie and letting her [Ella] shift for herself and I'm sure she is just as deserving. She has shown herself to be a hard worker and sensible in every way and got a second grade certificate all through her own efforts without any help from any one. I don't know what to say to Jim. He's getting dissatisfied and suppose he'll have any way in the fall. Firing [a job with the railroad, of maintaining a furnace fire to run a machine] is awful hard work and he'd never be able to stand it. Besides he'd find it hard work to a job of firing. I'm positive that it is best for him to stay at home but if he can't be made to believe it he'll be in misery if he has to stay there and work hard. If it had been Gods will that I could have got in with an honest man I might have been in a position to help them all out at home in a year or so but as it is it seems there's nothing but misery for all of us. I hear from Gertie quite often & she likes Dak & is doing well. Must close and am glad that you are happy any way. Write soon.

Bro Dick.

Dick finally resolved his angry feelings about the letter from Brennan, never abandoning Mollie as a confidante. He continued to write of their siblings' ambitions, commenting on Ella's wish to teach kindergarten and rejecting it as being "Protestant."

Como Station, July 14, 1889

Dear Sister Mollie,

I don't see any reason why you couldn't have sent me that letter in the first place as it would have given me an insight into what Brennan intended doing and also showed me a little clearer just what he is or just what the bookkeeper he speaks about is. He . . . knew before Brennan sold to me just the kind of man Donohue was and what he was and had been doing all the time.

As for him telling me that he was not doing what was right, he never said one word until I took charge of the books and found out, and as for my saying I did not care and that the business could go to the dogs, I said so after I had begged him to take the business back while there was some chance for him to save it and he had refused and the business was entirely ruined. This was but a few days before the store was closed by the sheriff and I saw that I was utterly ruined and was half crazy. He says too that he could have had the other six hundred dollars had he wanted it. He tried hard to get me to take up the notes with the money I had which belonged to Auntie Kate and yourself and offered to discount them $50 if I would pay them. I came awful near doing it too but something told me I had better not, and I thank God for it for I would have been in an asylum before this if I had lost that too. He has twisted the story of how we came to make the deal all out of shape too, to suit himself. I will not get a single cent out of it and all this talk will not do a particle of good so we will say no more about it for it drives me nearly mad every time I think of it.

Mollie I cannot possibly send you the rest of what I owe you now but will do so as soon as ever I can. Do you mean the other $100? Did you get an acknowledgement from John for the $100. I sent him?

I read a letter from Gertie a few days ago and she likes Dak better every day.

As for Ella, I don't think she had better study to be a Kindergarten teacher, for that is a strictly Protestant institution and I'm sure she would be asked to do things which she would not want to. I don't think she fully understands that such is the case or she would change her mind.

I'll return Bs letter to you as soon as can see him and ask him about some of the statements contained in it.

Regards to Henry.

Write soon.

Bro Dick.

In these last two letters, the Gogin family had entered the twentieth century, and Mabel, who was yet to be born when John Gogin wrote to his elder sister Mollie on her teaching skills, penned this letter to Ella and Gertie who had each staked tree claims in Dakota. Like her sisters and brother Dick before her, Mabel's twenty-one year old head is filled with social news but she too worked outside the home, although she was not in the classroom. Her comments on clerking for the two store owners, who were Jewish, starkly reveals the prejudice of the times.

Berlin, Jan 29,1901

Dear Sisters:

Ella's letter came today and relieved our anxiety and we are glad to know the "smallpox" scare is so soon over with and hope no more cases will occur. We are all well as usual, only I have a cold that keeps my nose

red and sore from blowing it so much. I caught it at the Waverly "*sitting
out dances*" Friday night. I didn't "sit out" very many tho, as so many of
"our" crowd was there besides others I knew, and I had a nice time. I
wore my "patent leathers" for the first time and they are O.K. to dance
in, after I padded the heels. It was *3 A.M.* when I got home.

Art and [his wife] Mame came down Sat. and it was so cold Sun.
that they couldn't go home, and as the cold continued Art went on Mon.
and left Mame 'til today when she went home with Tom Mack as he was
going to Pine River on business. She and Art visited at Macks Sun.
evening and took Gertrude and they were quite smitten on her. She
knocks Francis all out, altho he has one tooth thru ahead of her. She
grows "like a weed" and is just as good as ever, and *so cute.* It seems lonesome here without her. Mame was glad as the rest of us to hear that Gertie and Richard were coming and we hope you will not disappoint us.
Mother is "saving things up" for you already, so *don't miss it.* Well I've
launched quite suddenly into a *wage earner,* and feel elated over my success. I am *clerking* for Messrs. Clavon and Davis, the new proprieters of
Koch's old store, and you should see me hustle. I wouldn't have known of
it but Miss Kraege came over in the storm Sunday and "put me on" and
I was down there bright and early Monday and applied for a "job." I
asked $5.00 per week and he said he'd give me $4.00 and if I *did well* he'd
make it *$5.00* and I have my "evening off" tonight so have time to pen
this.

As cold and blustery as it was Mon the store was *full* all day and the
cashier told me they took in between $1100. and $1200.00, and the next
day the crowd was so big that they had to *lock the doors* for about 2 hrs in
the P.M. Today the crowd was not so big but we had a better chance to
sell, so took in just as much. I am doing *fine* so far and like it very much,
but of course we get pretty tired. Have to work 'til 9:30 every night so far,
but our employers are very nice men to clerk for *I* think, even they *are
Jews.* I have had nice customers the most of the time, and one old lady
whom I did not know, complimented me highly [in hearing of the
"boss") on being so nice to her, and said she'd "look me up" if she came
in again. We have 12 clerks P.M.'s and then don't have enough. Mame
Rhellan clerks there too and is a jolly good girl.

Feb 2nd. Well I was interrupted by the arrival of Martin, and went
to the card social with him, and haven't had a moments time since to fin-
ish my letter. I had no chance to take any-thing for the lunch; so we had

to go to the bakers and buy a cake. I had my purse but Martin wouldn't let me pay for it. There was but *one* other cake at the hall, all bread and butter, and they had to buy some. We were late, but I had fine success and won 8 games. There was 18 tables full so you see what a crowd we had. It was announced that night that there would be an "old fashioned dance" Friday night, and M. said he'd come if he could, so I told him to call for me at the store. I waited for him there but as he didn't come I started out, and went to the hall *alone[.]* There was a *big* crowd again and I had all the dancing I could stand as I was pretty tired. I had to wait 'til the girls went home so it was 1:30 when I got home; and I was at the store at 8 next morning and held out allright during the day. Mr. Dulliver introduced me to a nice little grocery agent and I had a waltz and quadrille with him. He was an excellent dancer.

Well I finished my "job" at the store last night, as they were pretty well sold out and didn't need any extra clerks now; and just think! He paid me *$6.00*, without saying a word about our previous agreement. He paid each of us $1.00 per day, which I think pretty good for "green hands." He also took down my name and said he might send for me some other time. We had to work very hard the first 3 days but the last 3 were dull ones and we were not so busy. I like the work so much better than I ever thought I would, but then I was fortunate in getting only a few *tough customers;* and I held my own with *them,* and made them pay all they should. My 'partner' is still here, and we managed to "make connections" a few times. He *"swore up and down"* he was coming up to the dance Friday night, and engaged a twostep, and tho I didn't let him think so, I half believed he'd come. I saw him when I was dancing with Ed Fitz. standing down on the corner with another fellow, watching the dancers, and if he'd come up *then* I'd have gone home with him but he didn't, and I guess it was just as well as I suppose they'd all think it was a "put up job." I was provoked at him tho, so when he overtook me next morning and asked if I "felt like 30 cents." I turned on him and called him "an old *fraud"* He had to stop at Stubbee just then and asked me to "wait a minute" but I snapped out "I won't, I'm mad at you" and piked right along. I haven't seen him since. I suppose I was rather hasty, but then, I hate to be lied to by any one I like.

Today has been *very* cold. I went to early mass, and again tonight as we had our installation of officers at 7:30 (and I am treasurer) and after Benediction, the blessing of throats as tomorrow is St. Blaze's day.

Mother went to high mass and Mrs. Basiring made her stay there to dinner and spend the P.M. and she had a big time. Martin called to tell me
he'd try to be on hand Thurs. night to take me to the . . . Ball. I told him
I hoped it would be warmer as all the girls were going to wear light
dresses and he said, "O my! Don't be so foolish" etc. so I asked if I might
wear his fur coat. He said yes, and then as he was outside and far enough
away to be *courageous*, he said "you may have the *sleeve of this one*," and
then ran. He's getting braver tho, and takes my arm now, like a little
man. He invited me to go to Wautoma with him last week but I couldn't,
and he didn't go either and don't know if he'll go later or not. If it were
only good sleighing I'd enjoy going. He was going on business and that it
would be pleasanter to have company. I told him they'd think *sure* we
were going after the [marriage] *license*, and we had a good laugh over it.
Butters have a cousin (a girl) visiting them and they want me to go with
them up to Mame's this week, but as I did not see 'em today I don't know
when they'll go. We had a letter from Dick this week and he is to spend
the rest of the winter at Wilmar Minnesota as agent. You should have addressed him at West Superior as I told you. If you send the package to
Wilmar now he will get it. He said he hadn't heard from you but that it
was his own fault. Well I must close. We received Gertie's letter today.
Richard is right in preferring to come *here* and you must not think of dis-
appointing him. How soon can you come? With love to all from all.

    Thanks for the papers.

    Mabel

*Mabel penned this final letter, but as "Auntey Mabel" writing to the next genera-
tion, Charlotte Boyd, Mollie's daughter. The topic was perhaps one of the most
common: toothache and the dentist. Although the letters ended with talk of the farm
and horses, Mabel also mentioned a car, indicating that the Gogin family, despite
the various problems each individual had withstood, had done well.*

                                    Berlin, June 24, 1908

Dear Charlotte,

    Your nice long letter came Monday and was much appreciated, as it
found me in *"deep distress"* and caused me to smile and forget my troubles
for a time at least. It seems there is no rest for the wicked, and I guess I
must be pretty bad. Martin was home all last week, working in Berlin as
they couldn't get the right cement in Wautoma 'til last Saturday. He re-

turned to Wautoma Monday morning, and I promised him I'd go slower this time and rest up, while he was away. Well, I haven't done much *work*, but I haven't exactly *rested* either, as I went down town Monday A.M. to see about my "jaw" which had been aching for about 4 days. I thought at first it was neuralgia but decided it must be my tooth as went to Dr. Huson the dentist and he pronounced it an ulcerated tooth. It was the 2nd tooth from the back on the lower jaw and the swelling which was slight was lower down. He thought he could treat it, so drilled out one of the fillings, (it had 2) and put some stuff in it. I went to Dollivers for dinner and staid there 'til after 2 o'clock and it ached so hard all the time. I went back to the Dr. again and he *lanced* the abscess, and *O my how it did hurt!* I came right home then and put hot applications on it the rest of the day and went to bed with the hot water bag. I was all alone as grandma went out to Currcans that morning, and you know how it stormed all night. My tooth ache bothered me worse than the storm and I never slept until after *3:30* A.M. I was just *sick* next day, but thought it would let up, so didn't call up Huson 'til about 3 P.M. and he told me to come down, but I replied that I wasn't able to, so he said he'd come up. He came about 5:15, and found he'd have to pull it, "altho he'd rather take a licking than do it." Mrs. Henderson happened to be here when he came and staid 'til the ordeal was over. She brought me in a nice dinner at noon, and was so good to me. Well he froze the old tooth and when he drew it out without breaking it, (as he feared) he uttered a very fervent *"Thank God."* It didn't hurt nearly as much as the lancing did, and I didn't even *whimper.* I slept like a top[?] all night last night, and feel much better today, but the abscess hasn't broke yet, and I have plenty of "cheek." I must wash tomorrow if I don't get any worse.

Martin has bought a 3 yr. old colt for $80.00 and taken it to Wautoma to break it in. He may not come home next Sat. Yes, I was disappointed at finding him gone when I reached Wautoma. I got off the train and found Ed's wife there and when she told me, I got aboard again. She wanted me to stay, any how, but I thought if he had been home long, I'd better come and see to things. My strawberries blighted and then the dry weather finished them, but the rest of my garden looks fine. My sweet peas are all budded, and I have one rose nearly opened. Gertie and I got home at 7:30 that night, from Omro. You see Dot thought the horses were afraid of the car so I hastened away to tie 'em and it took so long that when we came running back the car was just moving away, and of course Dot didn't see us. I was delighted to get her postal and know that she made connections all right as it would have been too bad to go to the extra expense of a livery and then not get any benefit. We enjoyed the trip *immensely*. I had a postal from [her sister] Annie but she didn't *say* anything on it. Am glad you are nearly there with your house-cleaning and I'll bet it looks fine.

Lovingly, Aunty Mabel.

FOR FURTHER READING

Dezell, Maureen. *Irish America: Coming into Clover: the Evolution of a People and Culture.* New York : Doubleday, 2001.

Diner, Hasia. *Erin's Daughters in America: Irish Immigrant Women in the Nineteenth Century.* Baltimore: Johns Hopkins University Press, 1983.

Hintz, Martin. *Irish Milwaukee.* Images of America Series, Arcadia: 2003

Foster, R. F. *Modern Ireland: 1600–1972.* New York: Penguin Books, 1989.

Kenny, Kevin. *The American Irish: A History.* New York: Longman, 2000.

Kinney, Thomas P. *Irish Settlers of Fitchburg, Wisconsin 1840–1860.* Fitchburg Historical Society, 1993.

McCaffrey, Lawrence J. *The Irish Catholic Diaspora in America.* Washington, D.C. : Catholic University of America Press, 1997.

McDonald Grace. *A History of the Irish in Wisconsin in the Nineteenth Century.* New York : Arno Press, 1976, c1954

Miller, Kirby, A. *Emigrants and Exiles: Ireland and the Irish Exodus to North America.* New York: Oxford University Press, 1988.

Moody, T. W. and F. X. Martin, *The Course of Irish History.* Cork : Published in association with Radio Telefís Éireann by Mercier Press, 2001.

This book depends first and foremost on letters, diaries, and short autobiographies found in archives at the Wisconsin State Historical Society. Anyone looking to explore more about the Irish in Wisconsin would do well to start their research in the Historical Society, whose staff is both helpful and knowledgeable.

INDEX